D0108384

OTHER TRUE RESCUES AT SEA BY MICHAEL J. TOUGIAS

The Finest Hours:
The True Story of a Heroic Sea Rescue

A Storm Too Soon:
A Remarkable True Survival Story in 80-Foot Waves

Into the Blizzard:
Heroism at Sea During the Great Blizzard of 1978

THE TRUE RESCUE CHAPTER BOOK SERIES

True Rescue: The Finest Hours

True Rescue: A Storm Too Soon

ATTACKED AT SEA

ATTACKED AT SEA

A TRUE WORLD WAR II STORY OF A FAMILY'S FIGHT FOR SURVIVAL

An adaptation for young readers of *So Close to Home: A True Story of an American Family's Fight for Survival During World War II*

MICHAEL J. TOUGIAS AND ALISON O'LEARY

Christy Ottaviano Books

Henry Holt and Company

New York

To the Downs Family: Ray, Ina, Lucille, Terry, and Sonny

Henry Holt and Company
Publishers since 1866
120 Broadway
New York, New York 10271
mackids.com

Henry Holt books may be purchased for business or promotional use. For information on bulk purchases, please contact Macmillan Corporate and Premium Sales Department at (800) 221-7945 x5442 or by email at specialmarkets@macmillan.com.

Library of Congress Cataloging-in-Publication Data

Names: Tougias, Mike, 1955-author. | O'Leary, Alison, author.
Title: Attacked at sea : a true World War II story of a family's fight for survival /
     Michael J. Tougias, and Alison O'Leary.
Other titles: So Close to Home (Young reader's adaptation) | True World War II
     story of a family's fight for survival
Description: New York : Christy Ottaviano Books; Henry Holt and Company, 2020. |
     Series: True rescue series ; 4 | An adaptation for young readers of So Close to Home: A True Story of an
     American Family's Fight for Survival During World War II." | Includes bibliographical references. | Audience:
     Ages 9-14 | Audience: Grades 7-9 | Summary: "A riveting WWII account of survival at sea-Book 4 in the
     True Rescue series from Michael J. Tougias, the author of the New York Times bestseller The Finest Hours."—
     Provided by publisher.
Identifiers: LCCN 2020009862 | ISBN 9781250128065 (hardcover)
Subjects: LCSH: Downs family. | Downs, Raymond, Sr.—Family. | Heredia (Ship) |
     World War, 1939-1945—Naval operations—Submarine. | Shipwreck survival—Mexico, Gulf of. |
     Survival at sea—Mexico, Gulf of. | U-506 (Submarine) |
     World War, 1939-1945—Naval operations, German.
Classification: LCC D744 .T58 2020 | DDC 940.54/51—dc23
LC record available at https://lccn.loc.gov/2020009862

First Edition, 2020

Printed in the United States of America by LSC Communications, Harrisonburg, Virginia.

10 9 8 7 6 5 4 3 2 1

CONTENTS

PROLOGUE

World War II began when Nazi Germany invaded Poland in 1939 and Great Britain and France tried to halt the Nazi take-over of Europe. At that time the United States had not joined in the war. Tensions were high not only between the United States and Germany but also between the United States and imperial Japan. Like Germany, Japan had been invading other countries. The United States responded by not selling Japan any more oil. This was a serious blow to Japan, which imported 90 percent of its oil.

Despite the embargo, Japan refused to withdraw its troops from countries it had invaded. Japanese leaders believed that war with the United States would break out sooner or later. They decided that their best chance to win this war would be by striking first. Japan did that in a surprise attack on the U.S. Naval Base at Pearl Harbor in Hawaii on December 7, 1941.

Three days after Japan bombed Pearl Harbor, Nazi Germany also declared war on the United States. (Germany, Italy, and

Japan—the main Axis powers—were engaged against the Allied nations, which included Great Britain, the United States, and the Soviet Union, in World War II.) One of the first acts taken by German leader Adolf Hitler against the United States was to send German submarines, called U-boats, toward American shores.

The U-boat commanders were instructed to take the war to North America and told that more U-boats would follow to ramp up the attacks. The detailed orders, written by Vice Admiral Karl Dönitz, gave the U-boat commanders the freedom to torpedo any large U.S. ship they came across. By sinking any big ships, including merchant ships in addition to U.S. Navy ships, Germany would hurt the entire U.S. war effort. This strategy would also reduce America's capacity to transport fuel and supplies to its ally Great Britain and to strike back at Germany.

Each U-boat would keep track of the approximate tonnage of the ships it sank so that Dönitz and Hitler could measure the success of the plan. Called Unternehmen Paukenschlag, or Operation Drumbeat, the mission would bring devastation to the doorstep of the United States.

The United States was ill prepared to defend itself against the U-boats, even though the British—who had cracked the Enigma machine the Germans used to send coded messages—gave ample warning. The U.S. Navy had most of its limited resources deployed in the Pacific and had done little to prepare for the U-boat onslaught. Many coastal cities ignored blackout requests, while navigational buoys and lighthouses shone brightly, helping the enemy enter shipping lanes and establish positions for spotting ships. American freighters and tankers also traveled alone in coastal waters, rather than in convoys or groups, protected by warships. Many ships remained lighted and frequently used their radios, which the Germans monitored.

U-boat commanders could not believe their good fortune when they surfaced at night and saw the clear silhouette of a ship steaming by. Often, there were multiple targets to choose from, and commanders had to decide which one to home in on first.

U-boats sank approximately 170 ships off the eastern coast of North America and in the Caribbean in just four months, from January through April 1942. Finally, in May 1942, the United States improved aircraft surveillance of German subs while also experimenting with the convoy system. These changes, however, were employed only along the East Coast. Admiral Dönitz responded by simply diverting some of his subs to the Gulf of Mexico, where the good hunting could continue.

Two U-boats, U-506 and U-507, were the first to head toward the Gulf. Commanding U-506 was Erich Würdemann, a young and daring opponent who had shown considerable skill. Würdemann's hunt would take him deep into the Gulf, just off the coast of New Orleans, Louisiana, and toward a freighter, the SS *Heredia*, which carried the Downs family of San Antonio, Texas. This is the story of that family, U-boat 506, and what happened when their paths intersected on a May night in 1942.

PART I

"*Some experts think that if Hitler had had fifty more U-boats in 1939, he would probably have won the last war.*"
—WOLFGANG FRANK, *THE SEA WOLVES*

A TIRED OLD WORKHORSE

Eight-year-old Raymond "Sonny" Downs Jr. was disappointed by the drab gray freighter called *Heredia* looming above him at a port in Costa Rica. Sonny had steamed from the United States to South America 11 months earlier aboard a cruise liner with all the comforts of a five-star hotel. Now, on May 12, 1942, his return trip to the States would be aboard the *Heredia*. She was an old ship that primarily transported produce rather than pampered passengers. The big difference, however, between his earlier voyage and the one he was about to embark on was the risk. The United States had entered World War II five months earlier, and Germany had sent its U-boats toward the Americas for what they considered easy "hunting."

Sonny was aware that war had broken out, but at this moment he was more intrigued by the giant cargo nets full of bananas that were being loaded onto the *Heredia*. He and his 11-year-old sister, Betty Lucille, who preferred the name Lucille over Betty, ran up the gangplank to the ship's deck. From this vantage point they had a better view of the stevedores, the workers who loaded the vessel, stowing the cargo below.

Brown-eyed Lucille, who had a dimpled chin and stood a full head taller than Sonny, hadn't known there were this many bananas in all of Costa Rica and Colombia, where they had been living the past few months. Other workers were loading heavy sacks onto the ship. Sonny, never shy, asked a senior crew member of the *Heredia* what was in the sacks.

"Coffee, young man," said the sailor. "All bound for the U.S."

"We thought so," said Lucille. "We thought we could smell coffee."

"Well, you're too young for coffee, but would you two like a Coke?"

"You bet!" exclaimed Sonny.

"Okay, follow me to the galley."

Lucille shouted down the gangplank, telling their parents they were going to the galley, where meals were prepared and served. The two kids skipped away, Sonny barefoot. *Maybe this trip is going to be a good one*, thought Sonny. *It doesn't matter how old the ship is if the crew is nice.*

Sonny was correct: It wasn't every day that children were on board the freighter, and the crew was more than accommodating.

In fact, only six of the 62 people aboard the ship were civilian passengers. Six others were members of the navy, assigned to man the guns mounted on the highest deck. The rest of the people on board were crew members. And, yes, the 4,700-ton *Heredia* had steamed many a mile since she'd been built 34 years before, in 1908. Powered by an oil-burning engine that turned a massive propeller, the steel ship was 378 feet long and had a large funnel that belched black smoke from the burned fuel.

Although the vessel was originally a passenger ship named the *General Pershing*, it had been converted to a freighter by the United Fruit Company and renamed *Heredia*. Most of its former elegance had been worn away by time and rust, and now it was a tired old workhorse. But as Sonny and Lucille Downs bounded after the crewman toward the galley, they couldn't wait to get underway and explore every inch of the freighter. The journey was expected to last seven days before they reached New Orleans, Louisiana.

~

The children's father, Raymond Downs Sr., worked as a railway steam engine mechanic for the United Fruit Company in Colombia and Costa Rica, South America. He, too, looked forward to the voyage and a return to the States. When Japan had bombed Pearl Harbor, Ray had decided it was time for him and his family to leave South America and return home. At 36 years old, he was hoping to join the U.S. Marines. Ray was certainly in good enough shape to fight. He was six feet tall and weighed

200 pounds, with plenty of upper-body strength and unending stamina. His fit condition, coupled with his dexterity and quick fists, made Ray a formidable opponent should anyone underestimate him in a challenge.

Ray lived life in a straightforward, no-nonsense manner and taught his kids that if they worked hard, good things would come. That mindset had served Ray well, and his job with United Fruit in Colombia had paid handsomely. Now, however, he was anxious to get home and be a part of his country's response to Japan's sneak attack. Like many young men at the time, Ray had patriotism running high in his veins. He wanted to see his family secure in their hometown of San Antonio, Texas, before he joined the military.

Sonny had some of his dad's characteristics, showing athletic promise even at a young age and sharing a competitive and determined nature. But while Ray, with his close-set eyes, had an intense, even threatening, look about him, Sonny usually wore a wide, welcoming smile. The boy would strike up a conversation with anyone nearby. He had tremendous respect for his father but recognized that his dad was set in his ways and often unyielding. Sonny knew better than to try to argue with him.

When Ray announced that the family was going to leave South America, Sonny hadn't been happy, but he didn't question his father's decision. Instead, he told his mother, Ina, that he wanted to stay right where they were because he was having fun. Ina, however, was in complete agreement with her husband, although for a different reason.

Ina Downs was a beautiful woman who was every bit as strong-willed and opinionated as her husband. While she understood Ray's desire to return home with a war underway, the 33-year-old mother's primary concern was her children's well-being. Besides Sonny and Lucille, she and Ray had a third child, 14-year-old Terry, who was living back in the United States with his grandparents. Terry had made the trip with the family to South America but had stayed only a couple of months before returning to Texas to continue his schooling.

Ina missed Terry terribly. She also felt out of place in South America, as she didn't quite fit in with either the locals or the other Americans who worked for United Fruit. Even before the war broke out, she had broached the subject of returning home, especially after she observed a couple of wild parties hosted by other American workers. It bothered her that excessive drinking was happening all around them while she was trying to raise Sonny and Lucille with strong values.

Now, as Ina looked up at the towering gray hull of the ship that would take them home, she said a silent prayer that her family would be safe. Reliable news about the German U-boat threat had been hard to come by, but she knew of a couple of attacks in the Caribbean and off the east coast of Florida. She was unaware of any attacks in the Gulf of Mexico, through which the family would be traveling. Like most people, she assumed the Gulf was out of U-boat range.

Ina reflected on the months the family had spent in Colombia and Costa Rica, and despite her desire to leave, she did not regret the experiment of living abroad or her husband's decision to take a job there. His position at the United Fruit Company had enabled them to save a considerable sum of money, which was sorely needed. That money, along with their furniture, personal belongings, and car—all their earthly possessions—was being loaded onto the *Heredia*. Prior to Ray's job in South America, the family had struggled financially. But now they were returning home in good shape and might even be able to buy a house. *When we came down*, Ina thought, *we barely had two nickels to rub together, so the grand adventure was worth it.*

Ina let her mind drift back to the beginning of the journey . . .

2

INA AND THE SOUTH AMERICAN VENTURE

(SEVERAL MONTHS EARLIER)

There was so much to do to prepare for the year in South America: digging up birth records, sewing travel outfits for the growing boys and Lucille, saying goodbye to friends at church.

No one in Ina's immediate family had had a passport before. Yet she had confidence that she'd clear all the hurdles, from gathering the children's birth certificates to getting documents from relatives swearing to her and Ray's own birth dates. Getting passport photos of the family taken meant pressing clean clothes and going downtown to a studio, where the photographer stood under the hood behind a large black camera. She only hoped to get the children home and changed into their play clothes before anything happened to the Sunday outfits they wore for the picture.

The passport photos caught the family in an adventurous mood, the children smiling brightly behind their young mother, the boys with their hair slicked to one side. Their resemblance to their father was unmistakable, but Ray's photo showed him unsmiling, even grave. Perhaps his brow was knit with the weight of the decision to move his family to another country. Sitting for a photo was something they'd done only once or twice before, so the children knew it was an important occasion.

For Ina, a hardworking Texas girl, redundant organizing her family's papers and possessions was a welcome distraction from thinking about being away from home for more than a year. In letters, she tried to reassure her parents about the decision to move to Colombia; in the process, she was reassuring herself as well. She'd never been far from her home state before, not even across the great Mississippi River.

Ray and Ina put great faith in United Fruit as their ticket to the future. They hoped to own a home on a nice lot and drive a newer car someday. They knew Ray had the ability and the skills to succeed as a railroad mechanic; he just needed an opportunity to prove himself. At night, the couple talked quietly about Ray's new job and the upcoming adventure.

For Ina, arriving at their South American home would be like winning the lottery. They'd been told that United Fruit would provide them with a home that featured a dining room, a kitchen with an electric range and a refrigerator, two bedrooms, a bathroom, and a laundry room. And the company would try to find them an even larger home over the coming months so that there would be plenty of room for the children. Ina laughed when she first heard that news: *If only they could see how we live now!*

Indeed, the family home in San Antonio was a bit cramped and always humming with activity. Lucille had the second bedroom, and the boys shared a large storage room as their bedroom. But there was always space for Ina to spread out her sewing—she made most of the kids' clothes, in addition to sewing for her employer, a costume shop.

It wouldn't be easy for the children to leave the home they'd known all their lives, Ina knew, and she worried about it. On Denver Street, they roamed freely with other children after school. Terry, then 13, had a job sweeping up in the store down the block, as well as selling copies of *Liberty* magazine to neighbors for a nickel apiece. Lucille tagged along with him when he delivered one of Ina's fresh-baked pies to a customer. And the boys in the neighborhood knew that Lucille, a girl tall for her age, could keep up with them in running races and stickball games. Denver Street would be hard to duplicate in far-off Colombia.

The family packed up in early June and left San Antonio with only the things they needed. It was nearly a day's drive to Ina's parents' home in Gainesville, Texas, where the kids tearfully left the family dog, named Boy. While Ina's parents were saddened to see the family leaving for such an extended period of time, they knew Ina and Ray had to follow the money and job opportunity south. They stood on the porch and waved the young family goodbye, holding back their emotions as best they could. The house seemed small and quiet after the tumult of the children's voices and energy.

~

Before Ina's dream home in South America would become a reality, the family had a rough trip to the port in New Orleans. "Everything seemed to go wrong," Ina wrote to her parents. First, the sky opened up and it rained in sheets, dampening everyone's spirits. In Huntsville, Texas, the car broke down and Ray had to get out in the rain and fix it. They stayed the night with friends and in the morning discovered a flat tire. There was another blowout on the short drive from Houston to Beaumont. Then a racket began coming from the car's engine near the state line, making the car almost impossible to drive.

Limping into Louisiana, the Downses found the streets in the small town of Vinton quiet. Fortunately, they located an understanding Chevrolet mechanic, who allowed the bedraggled family to bring their car in at quitting time—5:00 P.M. The tired and dirty children, haggard parents, and worn-out car had been treated roughly by the road, so the mechanic agreed to set things right. He got to work immediately, with Ray watching over his shoulder while Ina fed the children from a picnic basket in the office.

When the mechanic was finished, it was midnight. As Ina packed the sleepy little ones back into the car, Ray settled up.

They'd need extra tires, because flats were a regular part of travel, and the family had a schedule to keep. But the $12.45 in repairs and new tires was more than Ray could pay out of pocket, so he asked the mechanic if the man would take his wristwatch for a portion of the bill. It was agreed, and he slid it off over his hand while Ina looked away through tear-filled eyes. But she set her jaw and got back in the car before they drove off into the night. Everything would work out fine once they got to Colombia.

By morning, the family was worn out from travel but awakened to lush green surroundings that were unlike most of what they knew in Texas. The wide brown Mississippi came next, and the kids stuck their heads out the windows to get a glimpse as they crossed it on the giant Huey P. Long Bridge. A sense of excitement grew in Ina and Ray as they realized the adventure they'd talked about and planned for was really beginning. New Orleans wasn't much farther down the road.

Once in the city, their excitement mounted further. Ray returned from the United Fruit offices with information about their trip: They were leaving immediately for Cristóbal, Panama, on the SS *Santa Marta*. The trip would take six days, and then there would be a layover of five days until a second ship took them to Barranquilla, Colombia, where they'd meet a plane for the final leg to Santa Marta.

United Fruit Company's "Great White Fleet" was a group of ships that operated between the Gulf States and South America, transporting employees, paying passengers, and cargo. The ship the Downses sailed on initially was a luxury liner of sorts. This was a huge departure from their everyday lives in Texas, and it made them feel valued and pampered by Ray's employer. Indeed, they were living like movie stars, if only briefly.

"They put us in Suite B, the Bridal Suite," Ina wrote to her father. "Ain't that something. I have to pinch myself every once in a while to realize this is me."

The family was among 89 passengers, many going to Havana, Cuba, or Panama to work for the government; some were just on a cruise. Fortunately, there were a few other children aboard, and Sonny found a boy about his age with whom he could roam the decks.

Terry and Ray watched with interest as a smaller pilot boat guided the big ship through the ever-changing sandbars at the mouth of the Mississippi. Once they reached the open water of the Gulf of Mexico, the Mississippi's muddy flow disappeared a little at a time until the water beneath them was aqua green. The pilot then left the bridge of the *Santa Marta*, descending a rope ladder on the side of the ship to his own boat. He waved to the passengers as the big liner slowly slipped by, leaving land behind.

Ina and Ray stood by the rail, mesmerized by the crystal-clear water. Soon they spotted movement in the ocean near the bow of the boat and called the children over to see. Dolphins were racing alongside the boat, arching up out of the water and seeming to swim on top of one another. There were so many new things to experience that the family forgot any worries about moving far from home.

Unfortunately, their enjoyment of the luxury of the cruise ship did not last long. Once the ship was deep in the Gulf, it pitched and rolled continuously, and the effects of the vaccinations everyone had received in New Orleans were being felt. Ina spent two days lying down, and other members of the family stayed close to their suite. During the layover in Cristóbal, Panama, the tropical heat was oppressive, making their stay less than festive.

In Colombia, United Fruit and similar companies had developed whole towns of workers, supplying nearly everything the families needed to keep productive for the organization. Started some 50 years earlier as a railroad company, its founders realized they could make a considerable profit by exporting bananas to the United States. These founders, nicknamed "banana barons," quickly became the largest employers in several countries of Central America, influencing governments and even running the postal service in one country. With hundreds of miles of railroad used to transport employees and fruit, men with skills like Raymond's mechanical knowledge were key to keeping things running smoothly for United Fruit. Dozens of ships either owned by or leased to the company regularly moved both employees and products.

Growing bananas requires tropical heat, and it was difficult for Ina to adjust to the oppressive humidity once they settled into the company town. But the heat and humidity didn't keep the kids from playing with new friends or exploring their surroundings deep in a lush jungle. They felt like royalty, with a sparkling new home, servants, and a well-paying job for Ray. The children stared in wonder the first time a man came by to leave a giant bunch of bananas on a hook outside the kitchen, as he did weekly for every household in the village.

The novelty of having hired help quickly faded for Ina, as did her energy, sapped by the heat and lack of purpose. "I don't have to do a thing all day—just dress and go to eat," she wrote to her parents. "A maid does the cleaning and we eat at the clubhouse and I have a laundress who washes and irons for me."

While Raymond had work to attend to, Ina's isolation was made more challenging by the difficulty in connecting across cultural barriers. Missing news from home, Ina was particularly homesick after a minor but painful foot injury. The family didn't have a radio, no newspapers were available, and letters were few and far between. It was difficult for Ina to make the transition from a busy San Antonio household to a daily routine of reading and simply directing the maids' work and shopping. She disliked the United Fruit community's lack of religious observance and other lifestyle differences that didn't match her view of a family-friendly environment.

During one holiday break, Ray took part in a company softball game and was quickly recognized as a strong athlete, but the fun went a little too far. While the whole family cheered as Ray slammed a home run with two men on base, winning the game for his team, the holiday cheer didn't end there. After the game, the other employees had a cocktail party, dinner, and dancing until the wee hours. Ina didn't need an excuse not to dance, as her foot was in a splint, but the excessive alcohol at the party rubbed her and Ray the wrong way.

Ina poured out her frustration in a letter to her parents: "The people here are mostly English. They are rather hard to understand and I find some are snobs. They are all very, very friendly in a distant sort of way. They give you the feeling you are on the outside looking in and you are classed according to your husband's job. If things don't change we are not staying any longer than our contract calls for."

While Ina and Ray felt like fish out of water among the employees of the company, the children adjusted quickly. Terry and Sonny figured out that the company clubhouse was a source of a sweet soda drink called a lime rickey, which they thought was free for the asking. But Ray got the bill and caught them at the clubhouse one day, acting like a couple of rich kids. He shooed the boys home and admonished them against bellying up to the bar for "free" drinks again.

Other parents informed Ina that school in the United Fruit colony wouldn't be rigorous enough for Terry. Most families were sending their teens back to the States for high school. Ina and Ray decided to do the same, even though Terry was having a great time playing golf with some hand-me-down clubs and swimming and running with a crowd of other youngsters. Ina alerted her parents that he'd be sent back to Gainesville to live with them while he went to school. The 14-year-old was back in

Texas within a month, traveling by plane, train, and freighter ship alone through several countries and concluding the trip with a train ride from the port in New Orleans back to Texas.

Sonny and Lucille would have to make the best of living in South America without their big brother.

3

WAR WORRIES AND THINKING OF HOME

After Terry returned to Texas, Ina made renewed efforts to become more involved in her South American community. She learned to speak Spanish by trading lessons with a local woman, and she joined a group of women sewing woolen dresses for the British War Relief effort. She and Ray often visited a neighbor to listen to radio broadcasts of President Franklin D. Roosevelt's fireside chats and other news of the day. World events were discussed among the workers, particularly the British, who rarely dared to take a trip home. Their reluctance was due to the escalating German U-boat attacks, which made travel and trade by ship a perilous endeavor.

Just three months before Japan's attack on Pearl Harbor,

President Roosevelt had been preparing the country for the war by discussing a series of what he called unprovoked attacks on American ships by German U-boats. Although the United States hadn't entered the war, the country was actively supplying Great Britain not only with raw materials to support its manufacturing but also with ships to replenish its fleet. While the United States was officially neutral, these actions infuriated Germany.

~

The war was far from Santa Marta but never far from the minds of the people there. The local company manager invited Raymond and Ina to a fancy dinner party where funds would be raised to help the people in Great Britain during their time of need. Ina enjoyed the evening immensely, especially the opportunity to dress up. "Everything was very correct and nice," Ina wrote, explaining to her parents that the proceeds from games of rummy and horse racing were going to support the Red Cross in Britain.

Then things began to change for the couple in unforeseen ways. Sigatoka, a fungal disease that kills the leaves of banana plants, was rampaging through the plantations. United Fruit attempted to get the Colombian government to pay some of the costs of spraying the plants to keep them alive, but the government refused. This threat was followed by a hurricane that damaged the crop. The war also hurt the banana market; only American ships could then take produce out of the ports to markets in the States. Because of these issues, fewer workers were needed on the plantations. Employees were laid off or transferred to Costa Rica, and Ina anticipated a major shake-up in Ray's railroad department as a result.

Having a teen far away also occupied Ina's mind. In a letter to Terry, she scolded him for not working hard enough in school. After a sweet sentimental line or two about how much he was missed, she dug in with her real message: "I was not so proud of your grades. You have football on your mind instead of making very good grades," Ina wrote. "Football is fun but just remember you are going to school to equip yourself for a lifetime of work of some kind so make the most of your studies."

Ina was very concerned about getting money to her parents for Terry's care. She was impatient with the system of cashing out company stock to send support money home. Ina learned that the stock took a month to sell, and then taxes were discounted from the proceeds. It was another reason to be discontent with life in Colombia.

That problem was solved when the company's troubles with shipping, hurricanes, and plant blights prompted them to send Ray to Costa Rica after the family had spent several months in Colombia. "It's a much nicer country," Ina wrote, anticipating better conditions and a different class of people. Getting mail and other communications from home faster would be an added bonus in moving to Costa Rica.

Resettling on the west coast of Costa Rica awakened Ina's interest in travel, as she was entranced by their train's route along a mountainside. The ground was covered in almost every species of fern known, the world around them lush and green. As the train skirted the mountainside, she pointed out to Lucille and Sonny a valley far below them, where a mountain river hurried to the sea over huge boulders and rocks, with many beautiful waterfalls along its path.

The family's sense of wonder was piqued, and soon after arriving at their new home, they awakened at 3:00 A.M. to drive to the top of the Irazú volcano by sunrise. "I never dreamed I'd be able to gaze upon such a thing," Ina whispered to Raymond.

~

The December 7 attack by Japan's bombers on U.S. Navy ships and air bases at Pearl Harbor in Hawaii shattered Ina's newfound sense of well-being. Both she and Ray continually tried to learn more about the U.S. involvement in the war. Ina longed for a radio, to know more about the country's progress into war, so she and Ray could make a clear decision about their future. United Fruit's boats were being taken by the government and put into military service. The U.S. government also tightened access to the Panama Canal and gave warships priority, further limiting the fruit trade. The uncertainty ate at the couple, and Ray's desire to join the Marine Corps grew by the day.

"We aren't satisfied with this life to bring up babies in it," wrote Ina to her parents. "There is so much drinking going on and other things and Lucille is growing by leaps and bounds. It is not a healthy environment for a growing child. Ray is anxious to be doing something for the government, and feels he should offer his services in some way."

A month after this letter, Ina and Ray made their final decision: They would leave South America and return to Texas. United Fruit secured passage for the family on the *Heredia*.

A week before boarding, Ray was asked to sign a waiver releasing the company from all blame should their ship be attacked by a U-boat. Ray and Ina readily agreed, never imagining what was to come.

4

ADMIRAL DÖNITZ AND
HIS GRAY WOLVES

Sonny gazed up at the small deck on top of the *Heredia*'s wheelhouse and wondered at the machine guns mounted there, one on the starboard side and the other on the port side. His parents had told him they were for defense against German submarines. Ever curious, Sonny later found the captain and questioned him about the weapons. "Well, young Downs, the ones mounted at the top of the ship are machine guns, and the ones mounted on the bow and stern are a bit more powerful. Those are twenty-three-caliber, three-inch cannons." Sonny wanted to fire one, but knowing that was out of the question, he thanked the captain and ran off to tell Lucille what he had learned.

Captain Erwin Colburn, originally from Somerville,

Massachusetts, was personable and approachable. Red-haired and fair-skinned, the captain usually had a pipe in his mouth and always dressed in a crisp white uniform and captain's hat. Sonny liked the man; whenever their paths crossed on the ship, the captain had a kind word and the boy usually had a question. The crew was comprised of Americans and a few Filipino sailors. The Filipinos invariably wore their dark blue peacoats around the clock, even when Sonny was quite comfortable in his bare feet and shorts. Taking a cue from their captain, the crew was friendly and took the time to answer Sonny's and Lucille's many questions.

The men whom Sonny and Lucille didn't know well were the six members of the U.S. Navy Armed Guard, who rotated shifts manning the guns or scanning the horizon with binoculars. Sonny spent a considerable amount of time watching the men in uniform, hoping to see them at least fire a machine gun in a practice round. He knew his dad wanted to fight the Germans and Japanese, too, but the eight-year-old quickly concluded that the navy men had the most boring job on earth. All they did was stare out to sea, occasionally switching positions with one another to break the monotony.

After *Heredia* made a brief stop in Puerto Barrios, Guatemala, the Downs family settled into a routine as the ship plowed northwestward at a steady 12 knots. After breakfast each morning were emergency drills. An alarm would sound, and all on board were required to grab their cork-and-canvas life jackets, put them on and tie them tight, and then assemble at their assigned lifeboats. Because the Downses were passengers rather than crew, they were told that in the event of a real emergency, the crew would instruct them when to enter the lifeboats. The sailors would handle lowering the boats from deck level to the water.

Everyone was reminded by the captain and the officers not to drop anything overboard, lest they leave a clue for the Germans that a ship had recently passed. And all were instructed to immediately report any object they might spot in the water—it just might be a sub in the distance or even a periscope nearby. The captain also explained that the ship would mostly travel in a zigzag pattern to make it more difficult for U-boats to track the *Heredia* down. And although the captain could listen to incoming radio messages and alerts, he would not respond, because doing so might enable the enemy to find them. Lights on the ship, however, were not completely shut down at night.

Once the safety drills were over, the family had the rest of the morning and early afternoon free. Ray and Ina usually read, while Lucille and Sonny went exploring. Ina's joy at heading home was dampened by her unease about the U-boat threat. She was able to put it out of her mind during the day, but each evening she'd look out at the ocean, worried that a gray steel monster might rise up from the shadows of the swells. Ina knew that her fear was probably misplaced. Like most people, she believed the Gulf of Mexico was simply too far from Europe for a U-boat to reach. Ray had said the odds of a submarine finding the *Heredia* in this wide-open sea seemed near impossible.

Ina had heard rumors of an attack in the Florida Straits but tried not to dwell on it, because no other incidents had been reported. Along the East Coast of the United States, especially off Cape Hatteras in North Carolina. U-boat attacks were nearly common events. But that was a long distance from the Gulf. Ina also tried to remind herself that the *Heredia* was carrying bananas rather than oil or gasoline, which were the real quarry U-boats were after. Still, she'd feel a lot better when they safely reached New Orleans.

Ina's lack of knowledge about U-boats wasn't due solely to her having been far from home. Since the start of the war, the U.S. government had been controlling the information that was reported about U-boat attacks. By censoring the news, the government could keep the public from panicking about the number of ships sunk and from realizing the seriousness of the situation. Censorship couldn't keep a lid on all attacks—sometimes hundreds of civilians in waterfront communities witnessed horrific scenes of ships exploding. So while Ina worried about the possibility of an attack, she didn't fully realize that all merchant ships were easy targets for the U-boats, even *Heredia*.

Sonny and Lucille had no idea that their mother was worried; they were having too much fun. The children had complete run of the ship except for the ammunition room. The crew frequently offered them snacks and drinks, and it wasn't long before Sonny decided this voyage home was every bit as good as the trip to South America had been. He wished his brother, Terry, could have been with him and Lucille; Terry would have organized games and contests—competition that Sonny loved.

Two U-boats were in the Gulf of Mexico at the same time as the *Heredia*. U-507, commanded by *Korvettenkapitän* Harro Schacht, snuck into the Gulf via the Florida Straits on May 1, and U-506, commanded by *Kapitänleutnant* Erich Würdemann, followed on May 3. Their mission was simple: continue to sink as many American ships as possible. Their orders were to proceed toward the mouth of the Mississippi, where they might be able to send enough ships to the bottom to block river traffic. Schacht and Würdemann had plenty of leeway on where to operate, depending on the defenses they encountered and the opportunities they might find. But it was important to use their torpedoes wisely.

Like teammates, the two men had a friendly competition going to see who could sink the most large ships. Their success would be calculated in tonnage, the estimated weights of the vessels. The Germans knew that lives were lost in most of the attacks, but it was wartime, and this was their duty: to stop ships from delivering fuel, building materials, and even food.

The mastermind behind their movements was 4,500 miles away at the German navy's headquarters in Lorient, France, an area occupied by the Nazis. Admiral Karl Dönitz, age 50, was a tall, thin, tight-lipped, and serious man who worked tirelessly to extract maximum efficiency from his U-boats. He called his U-boats and crew "Gray Wolves" because the submarines were painted gray and the men often dressed in gray leather. Both the

U-boats and their crews were always on the prowl. Sometimes several submarines worked together like a pack of wolves to find the enemy and make the kill.

Lorient was just one of several U-boat bases among the French Atlantic ports on the Bay of Biscay, bordering Spain. The location made perfect sense; by leaving from France instead of from the German ports farther north, submarines could save fuel and travel time. Leaving from France also added 10 days of patrol in the Atlantic. To keep the U-boats safe from British airplanes while in port, an elaborate system of strong U-boat pens, like garages, was constructed. They looked like caves, with the tops and sides of the pens made of thick concrete and the doors three-foot-thick steel. Here, the U-boats were resupplied and repaired. Many of the pens had dry-dock facilities with slips for lifting a U-boat out of the water to inspect the hull. The Allies were well aware of the location of these pens and dropped tons of bombs on them, but little damage was done until the last year of the war.

The location of the pens enabled the German navy to keep constant pressure on the United States by sending fresh U-boats across the ocean as soon as tired crews returned home. The tactic was simple yet highly successful. From January to mid–April 1942, German torpedoes sank more than 170 ships but lost only one U-boat in American waters. And some of the easiest hunting was within five miles of the U.S. coast. Despite the U.S. government's efforts to limit news about the carnage, people who lived along the coast could guess what was happening. All sorts of debris washed ashore, including oil, broken lifeboats, life vests, and bundled supplies.

Americans who knew of the ships' sinkings wanted to stop the carnage, but they didn't want to be inconvenienced by the solution. When cities were told to follow blackout rules by turning off outdoor lighting (including signs and streetlights) at night, some people complained that it would be bad for local business. As a result, shore lights often burned brightly, even though it was well known that U-boats could use the illumination to their advantage to find ships that cruised near shore.

Finally, toward the end of April, improved defenses like patrol boats and submarine-spotting blimps began to make things more difficult for the U-boats off the eastern coast of the U.S. That prompted Dönitz to send a few U-boats to the Caribbean and the Gulf of Mexico, knowing that tanker ships full of oil traveled from refineries there. Without adequate fuel, neither the United States nor Great Britain could wage war effectively.

U-506 and U-507 were the perfect vessels to send into the Gulf because they were large, long-range submarines: 249 feet long, 22 feet wide, and equipped with 22 torpedoes, which could be loaded in six tubes (four at the bow and two at the stern). Three powerful guns were mounted on the deck and conning tower to repel aircraft and sometimes to sink boats when torpedoes were not available.

These submarines could dive to a maximum depth of 755 feet, protected by an outer steel hull and an inner pressure hull. Two nine-cylinder diesel engines powered the U-boat when it was traveling on the surface, recharging the enormous batteries for the electrical systems that ran the lights, radio, and electric motors. The batteries allowed the submarines to stay submerged for brief periods. While submerged, the vessel moved more slowly. It had to return to the surface periodically to both recharge the batteries (by running the diesel engines) and replenish its supply of fresh air. There were typically 52 crewmen aboard.

The range of the subs was an incredible 13,400 nautical miles when the vessel cruised on the surface at 10 knots. Its maximum surface speed was 18.3 knots, while the maximum submerged speed was 7.3 knots.

Another type of German submarine, which sailors called *Milchkühe* (milk cows), provided fuel and food like a floating dock, doubling the time the U-boats could stay at sea. The massive 1,700-ton milk cows met with U-boats at a secret spot in the ocean. A long hose carried the diesel fuel from the big resupply sub to the smaller attack sub as both sat on the ocean's surface about 150 feet apart. The milk cow also supplied fresh bread (from an onboard bakery), medications, and mail from Germany. These could be delivered to a submarine in a dinghy or on a raft. Sometimes the milk cow brought additional torpedoes. The big sub also removed sick or wounded crewmen. There were no torpedo tubes on the milk cows, and they were not designed to attack ships—their only weapons were antiaircraft guns.

The U.S. Navy didn't know about the milk cow submarines. Officials suspected that the Germans were receiving supplies from supporters in the United States and possibly from foreign ships. Rumors and speculation were rampant. Americans who lived along the coast believed that Nazi spies were in their midst. People were encouraged to watch for and report unusual behavior—like strangers visiting the beach without bathing suits and towels—that might indicate enemy submarines were getting instructions or support. Wild rumors circulated about German spies or U-boat crews coming ashore to gain important information about shipping. How else to account for so many American ships going up in flames?

~

In the first few months of 1942, most U-boats returned to Lorient unscathed and victorious after surprise hits on Allied vessels. During Operation Drumbeat, the U-boats were sinking ships faster than the Americans could build them. Oil shortages quickly became a problem for President Roosevelt and his war advisers. Civilian gasoline use was strictly limited so there would be enough fuel for the war effort in the Pacific, Europe, and Africa. Dönitz's plan was working.

President Roosevelt pressed U.S. Navy Fleet Admiral Ernest King to put protective convoys together faster. That was difficult for the admiral because the country was fighting in both the Pacific and Atlantic Oceans, and warships were stretched thin. In the years leading up to World War II, King had asked for more ships and aircraft, but his requests were ignored. Then in 1940 the United States gave the British 50 older navy ships in a trade deal that helped the British prepare for war but left the U.S. Navy shorthanded. Protecting ships off the East Coast with armed convoys was virtually impossible without the proper escort vessels. The situation was so serious that American leaders built a giant 1,200-mile pipeline to get heating oil from refineries in the South to homes and businesses in the Northeast.

~

Part of the success of the Gray Wolves can be attributed to the intense training all U-boat men and commanders were required to undergo, which emphasized that the entire crew had to operate perfectly. One person's mistake could be deadly for all. Dönitz wrote that "every man's well-being was in the hands of all and . . . every single man was . . . indispensable."

In fact, the fighting spirit of sailors aboard U-boats was so strong that they willingly gave up what few comforts they had to increase their patrol time off the U.S. coastline. They filled some of the drinking and washing-water tanks with fuel and sacrificed parts of their tiny living quarters to make room for more supplies.

When sailors aboard U-506 and U-507 headed to the mouth of the Mississippi River, they were going farther than any others had, with no knowledge of what they might encounter.

5

HARRO SCHACHT
AND U-507

Commander Harro Schacht (pronounced "Shot"), age 34, and his crew aboard U-507 were on high alert as they passed between Cuba and Florida on April 30. They had just crossed the entire Atlantic Ocean in 26 days and would soon be the first U-boat ever to enter the Gulf of Mexico. Spirits were high, and the men looked forward to engaging the enemy. They knew that by being the first of the German subs to enter the Gulf, they would have plenty of opportunities to sink American ships. The crew of U-507 liked their chances of being recognized by Dönitz as one of the best U-boats, with Schacht as their ace.

The most effective weapons fired by U-507 (and all U-boats) were torpedoes. The 21.5-foot-long cylinders included propulsion and guidance systems, a depth device, and a pistol that detonated the warhead. Perfect for daytime attacks, these torpedoes did not leave a trail of bubbles, so they could not be seen. Once fired from submarines, they could travel 5,470 yards at 30 knots per hour, but commanders preferred to be much closer to their targets to ensure a hit. Like American torpedoes, these had their share of technical problems, sometimes malfunctioning and missing their targets, failing to explode, or exploding too early.

In the Gulf of Mexico, U-507 found the sinking ships to be easy. Its targets were often slow merchant ships, alone in the water without navy airplanes protecting them. Incredibly, getting torpedoed was almost expected by sailors during that time. The crew of one ship that Schacht hunted down and sank in the Gulf of Mexico included sailors who just months before had spent 11 days adrift on a raft after the ship they had served on was sunk.

Another time, Schacht heard a ship's captain calling the navy on the radio to report an explosion he had seen, giving the location so navy planes could find U-507. Schacht immediately searched for the source of the radio report and found the tanker not far away on a zigzag course, trying to get away. That ship was quickly sunk, too. Then Schacht slowly headed toward New Orleans and the Mississippi River Delta, where there would be more hunting.

~

Erich Würdemann and his crew on U-506 would provide Schacht with competition in sinking the most Allied ships in the Gulf. Würdemann was less experienced, having graduated from submarine school less than a year earlier, in September 1941. But the 28-year-old *Kapitänleutnant* was a quick learner.

Photographs of Erich Würdemann always showed him with an intense look: thick black eyebrows shadowing penetrating eyes, his brow furrowed in concentration. He was a good-looking young man with black hair slicked straight back. The photos gave a sense that he was confident and hungry for success. Strangely enough, his searing stare, thick dark hair, and serious demeanor were eerily similar to the photos taken of Ray Downs, Sonny's dad.

When passing through the Florida Straits, Würdemann's U-boat was running against the strong eastward current. It cruised more slowly than its maximum surface speed of 18 knots and was in a vulnerable position, close to land-based aircraft. Nervous about being exposed so near to onshore defenses, Würdemann stationed four lookouts with binoculars on U-506's conning-tower bridge. Each would scan an assigned 90 degrees of ocean and sky, searching for both ships to shoot at and aircraft that would try to stop them.

Twice a lookout spotted a plane and shouted for a crash dive. Everything moved quickly. The lookouts on the bridge leaped through the conning tower's open hatch and slid down the ladder, landing seven feet below, inside the sub. Behind them, a crewman slammed the hatch closed and secured it against the ocean water.

Then engineers shut off the diesel engines and turned on electric motors. Vents were opened to let the air out of the ballast tanks so the vessel would descend deeper in the ocean. To quicken the sub's descent, all available crew dashed to the narrow bow of the vessel, adding their weight to assist its nosedive away from the surface. The crash dive was a race against time to submerge the U-boat before airplane pilots could see it and start dropping bombs. If just one crew member on the sub was slow to perform his task, it might mean the end for all of them.

In the second crash dive that day, the U-boat must have been located by the American aircraft, because Würdemann later wrote, "2 aircraft bombs at depth of 60 meters. No damage." So while American defenses in the Gulf were sorely lacking, Würdemann knew he and his crew could never let their guard down while on the surface.

For most of his voyage into the Gulf, Würdemann simply played it safe, spending daylight hours underwater while using the cover of darkness to proceed on the surface. At night, the low silhouette of U-506 made it virtually impossible for spotters on a ship or a plane to see it with the naked eye. Würdemann knew that in the darkness he could easily find ships that either kept their lights on or were silhouetted by lights from shore. Once a ship was located, the commander could get surprisingly close to the enemy.

Würdemann on the U-506 had a lot of catching up to do to match the seven ships sunk in the Gulf of Mexico by Schacht and U-507. For Dönitz and Hitler, Schacht's success was a series of incredible victories, but for the Americans it was an absolute disaster. It is not known whether the news of this carnage reached Captain Colburn on the *Heredia*, but if it did, he elected not to worry the Downs family with it.

THE GRAY WOLVES AND
THE *MISSISSIPPI*

Sonny and Lucille were in the galley eating ham-and-cheese sandwiches made especially for them. A senior crew member sat at their table, chatting with the two children. Sonny blurted out that he would probably become bored on the voyage.

"Why's that?" asked the sailor.

Lucille answered before Sonny could. "Because we've seen the entire ship, even where the captain does the steering."

"Well, have you seen the engine room?"

"No! Can we?" shouted Sonny.

"First get permission from your parents. And if they say yes, meet me back here in two minutes."

The children raced through passageways, down a mahogany

staircase that was one of the few ornate features left from the ship's earlier days as a passenger ship, and then onward to their parents' cabin. The tiny room had a bunk bed, a table, a chair, and a closet. A door led into a bathroom that the parents shared with their children, who had an identical cabin on the other side of the bathroom.

Finding their mother reading on the lower bunk, they told her about their invitation to see the engine room of the ship. Ina thought for a minute and then said, "If you stay right next to the officer who is taking you there, you may go." The kids raced away, shouting, "Thanks, Mom!"

Ina smiled and shook her head: Sonny and Lucille were so happy, so healthy. She couldn't wait to get home.

Once in the engine room, both children covered their ears from the deafening roar of the giant pistons hammering up and down. The room smelled of oil and grease. Sonny thought the sight of the enormous moving parts was like entering a cave where giants might live. When Lucille tapped him on the shoulder and shouted that it was time to leave, Sonny took one last look around so that he could tell his brother, Terry, exactly what he'd seen.

Sonny reluctantly climbed the steps up from the engine room and into the fresh air. Once on the deck, he raced off to find his father to explain how the ship was able to power through the seas. He located his dad lounging on a deck chair, enjoying the warm May sunshine. After Sonny described his adventure in the engine room, his dad said, "Well, I've got news for you. We just entered the Gulf of Mexico, and we're about halfway home. Won't be long before you get to see your brother and Boy."

Sonny had missed the dog as much as he had his brother. "Can't wait!" said Sonny. "And, Dad, do you think we can sleep on the deck again tonight?"

The prior day and night had been warm and the family had found their cabins stuffy, so the whole family had slept on reclining chairs topside. Sonny loved looking at the stars, which were so clear that they appeared closer than he'd ever seen them. A gentle breeze had kept him cool, and the periodic passing of the Navy Armed Guard on watch made him feel safe.

"I don't see why not," answered Ray. "It's another warm day."

"All right!" shouted Sonny. He skipped away, heading down to the galley for a soda. His mind raced ahead to another night under the stars when he could secretly pretend he was a pirate sailing to distant adventure.

~

The crewmen on U-506 and U-507 could merely dream of escaping the heat and humidity inside their iron capsules. Their only relief came at night, when it was safe to surface and open the vessel's hatch. Those lucky enough to have conning-tower duty enjoyed deep breaths of the salt air, giving a sigh of pleasure whenever a breeze cooled their perspiring bodies.

The crew inside the U-boat longed for relief from the heat and terrible smells after weeks at sea. The engines generated heat, and the ventilation system could never provide enough fresh air. The warm waters of the Gulf of Mexico, together with the engine warmth, often sent temperatures in the sub above 110 degrees.

Even if there hadn't been high temperatures or engine fumes, the air inside a U-boat would have been foul. Consider that 50 men had to share the narrow, confined space for months with no baths and only one toilet. (The second toilet space was used for storage.) The smell of unwashed bodies could make a person gag. The crew also had to contend with high humidity that kept their dirty clothes and bedding damp. Fresh food was consumed in the first weeks at sea, leaving the men canned items or moldy bread to eat. Sickness spread quickly in these conditions, making the stink even worse.

A sailor's rank did not earn him greater privilege or better conditions in the U-boat service. Even Erich Würdemann grew a long beard and had no more privacy than the lowest-ranking sailor beyond a thin curtain separating his bunk from the 24-hour operation of the vessel.

Still, young German men were proud to serve on U-boats. German newspaper articles glorified the feats that the U-boat crews performed, and special magazines were dedicated to their exploits. There were even baseball card–like photos of U-boat aces that people collected and a popular 1941 German action movie titled *U-Boat, Course West!* When U-boat crews returned home after a month or two at sea, they were treated like heroes.

During wartime, a young man's options were limited. Military service was required in Germany. Hitler sent millions of poorly prepared troops to distant battlefields for more than a year of unrelenting toil, unbearable cold, and terrible bloodshed. At least on a U-boat, a crew member felt important and shared a sense of camaraderie with his commander, a relationship unheard of in other branches of the service. On U-506 and U-507, uniforms were made optional in the heat of the Gulf, so the crew often dressed in shorts and T-shirts. Space was so cramped that even the lowest-ranking crew members often saw and exchanged a word or two with their commanders.

Four crewmen who had almost daily contact with the commanders were the first watch officer, who was also second-in-command; the engineer; the radio and hydrophone operator; and the navigator. The stations of these last three were located near the heart of the boat.

During a submerged attack, the U-boat commander also spent considerable time with the combat helmsman, who steered the sub, in the enclosed conning tower that rose above the flat outside deck. Here the commander had access to the attack periscope, which could be raised or lowered. A ladder led from this tiny tower up through a hatch to the outdoor bridge, where a railing encircled an antiaircraft gun. There was no radar aboard, so sailors found enemy ships by using the periscope, watching with binoculars on the bridge, or listening for the sound of ship propellers heard over the hydro-earphones. A voice tube on the bridge allowed communication with the radioman and the control room. In rough seas, men on the bridge wore steel safety belts tethered to the vessel, which just might save their lives if a wave swept over them.

The *Zentrale*, or control room, was just below the conning tower, and it was loaded with an array of gauges, valves, and meters and a gyrocompass. The electrical gear to control steering was housed there, as were the chart closet and a second periscope.

All crewmen on U–507 and U–506 were totally focused on their tasks and felt the weight of the responsibility. They knew it was an honor to be the first two U-boats sent into the Gulf, and they wanted to make Admiral Dönitz proud of his decision to entrust them with such a crucial mission.

~

Near midnight on May 10, Schacht and U–507 turned toward the mouth of the Mississippi. The night was still: hazy, cloudless, no wind. In the commander's war diary, a reader can feel his excitement: "Want to be there [the mouth of the river] in the morning [May 11], to operate the entire day off the entrance." He made good on his plan, prowling near the Mississippi's outlet into the Gulf. "Mississippi lights as in peacetime," Schacht noted in his log. "Frequent mist off the Mississippi. Dirty water gives good cover at periscope depth but bad listening conditions [the hydrophone could pick up the sound of propellers only with difficulty]. Boat is difficult to handle because of unaccountable drifts. Patrol by 2 PC-boats. Air patrol along main shipping." Adding to the risk,

U–507 was in shallow water, sometimes with as little as 20 feet between the keel of the sub and the ocean's bottom.

Schacht moved in and out of the river delta, noting that even several miles from the Mississippi, the water was murky with silt. The commander spent most of the daytime hours submerged so that the submarine could not be spotted by plane. Toward dusk he'd come up to periscope level. He would look around and if all was safe, he'd bring the vessel completely to the surface and use his diesel engines to both hunt his quarry and recharge the sub's batteries.

On May 12 at 2:00 A.M., Schacht "again entered the yellow Mississippi water." Just before dawn, he steered for the south passage into the river, dodging a small patrol boat. As the sun came up, U–507 submerged but continued a slow prowl at the mouth of the river. A short time later, he sighted a slow-moving mine-sweeper, and Schacht couldn't resist taking a shot with one of his precious torpedoes. The aim was off, and the torpedo passed by the minesweeper, exploding into the jetty at the southwest entrance to the river. Incredibly, nobody noticed, and boat traffic continued coming and going through the river channel at the Southwest Pass.

Schacht was excited to see potential targets all around, but the mighty Mississippi was difficult to maneuver in. The current, the shallow areas, and the ships' frequent turning were frustrating. Steering the U–boat was incredibly difficult because he was in the grip of the Mississippi's current, and Schacht was in a deadly game of cat and mouse with patrol boats and aircraft. "I have to run the periscope up and down," he recorded, knowing that keeping the periscope up for too long increased his risk of being spotted.

Later that evening, Schacht finally found what he was looking for. A large ship lay unmoving just outside the river mouth. It was a 10,000-ton turbine tanker named *Virginia*, carrying gasoline, with 41 crew members on board, floating unarmed and unescorted, apparently waiting for dawn to move up the river. It was the sitting duck Schacht had been seeking. He wasted no time maneuvering U-507 into firing position and launched a torpedo that sliced through the steel hull of *Virginia*'s port side. Members of the crew ran to their emergency stations in a state of disbelief that their ship had been hit by a U-boat.

Schacht, watching through the periscope, was also in a state of disbelief. The ship did not explode but barely shuddered, lying motionless on the surface. He fired another torpedo. This time he got his intended result: a direct hit to the engine room that caused the *Virginia* to burst into flames. Schacht noted that the tanker flew apart and burned in two sections, with the sea ablaze in a widening circle.

Surviving crew members later told the *Times-Picayune* newspaper of New Orleans that there was no time to launch lifeboats. Flaming oil spread around the stricken ship, and the men hurled themselves into the water. Those who were not burned to death on the ship or in the ocean tried to swim away from the inferno. Survivor Michael Kuzma showed real bravery when, despite burns to his face and arms, and without a life jacket, he supported two injured shipmates and helped them to a buoy. They hung on for two hours before being rescued. Twenty-seven of Kuzma's crewmates were not as lucky. They died horrible deaths by burning or drowning or both.

Schacht tempted fate by watching the *Virginia* burn, even though he could also see two patrol boats through his periscope. He lay in a precarious position in shallow water. Finally, he slipped away to a place where he could fully surface and recharge his batteries in the dark.

7

MOVING EVER CLOSER

Schacht had the prime pickings of target ships because he was the first U-boat in the Gulf and then outside New Orleans at the mouth of the Mississippi. Erich Würdemann, following behind, was likely growing frustrated. The submarine was dogged by a particularly persistent aircraft. The plane made visual contact with Würdemann's sub on the surface as the ship raced toward the Mississippi and New Orleans. The young commander ordered the usual crash dive, waited almost an hour, and then slowly resurfaced—only to find that the plane was still in sight, circling above. The pilot must have spotted the sub again, because Würdemann reported that the "aircraft again turns toward the boat," prompting the commander to dive once more. These cat-and-mouse games were helping educate the young commander. He was learning to balance the need to sink ships with the welfare of his crew.

Würdemann was prudent, but he certainly wasn't alarmed. While the Americans were getting better at locating subs, their navy and air force had a long way to go before becoming skilled at sinking them. From January, when Operation Drumbeat started, through the end of April, the United States had sunk a grand total of one U-boat (U-85), whereas the U-boats had sunk 173 ships off the U.S. coast and in the Caribbean. Almost every U-boat commander who operated near the United States was astonished by how easily they located defenseless ships to sink.

Part of the reason for the Germans' success was that their navy had been at war for many months, whereas the United States had entered the conflict just five months earlier. The Germans had experience sinking ships, while the U.S. Navy did not have recent wartime experience hunting subs. Another reason was that most of America's naval resources went to the Pacific, where Japan occupied more and more islands that were strategic for both countries. In fact, Japan began its invasion of the Philippines, where U.S. troops were stationed, immediately after the bombing of Pearl Harbor.

~

Erich Würdemann—knowing he had a golden opportunity with so many ships steaming unescorted—undoubtedly wanted to start sinking a ship a day to catch up to Schacht. On May 10, he glided undetected into the prime hunting ground of the shipping lanes off the mouth of the Mississippi. Here would be enough tankers and freighters for both commanders to take their pick.

Once, when surfacing at dawn, a lazy lookout on U-506 almost caused a catastrophe. Würdemann wrote that the lookout recognized an approaching aircraft too late because the plane "came out of the sun." Afterward the commander became more alert than ever, even at night.

Two days after a close call with a U.S. Navy aircraft that might have bombed his U-boat, Würdemann was back in business, finding easy targets. His war diary entry noted "multiple freighters and tankers with east or west courses in sight." Over the next few days, the young commander sank a tanker almost every day. On May 13, he sank the *Gulfpenn* while Schacht, just five miles away, torpedoed its sister ship the *Gulfprince* but was unable to sink it.

May 13 was also the day most newspapers were allowed to acknowledge that the Germans had arrived in the Gulf. On page 3 of the *Times-Picayune*, an article proclaimed AXIS SUBMARINES INVADE GULF AND INFEST THE ATLANTIC. The story said U-boats, which were described as "raiders," had "violated waters impregnable in the last World War." The newspapers reported only two ships sunk in the Gulf (although there had been many more), but they broke the silence regarding the terrible toll the Germans were inflicting. The delay and lack of detailed information was not the fault of the newspapers, but rather part of the U.S. Navy's strategy to use censorship to cloud the government's incompetence in fighting the U-boats.

~

Schacht and his crew on U-507 were running low on fuel and torpedoes, but they managed one last daring victory. Their victim was the *Amapala*, which had left New Orleans with mixed cargo and a complement of 57 sailors. At 4:30 P.M., the ship's lookouts spotted U-507 catching up with them on the surface. Captain Christiansen immediately radioed an SSS signal (the code for submarine attack) while he ordered the engines full steam ahead at 16 knots. The distress signal was heard by the radioman on U-507, and he in turn warned commander Schacht that airplanes would soon be on the scene with their bombs. Yet Schacht kept his submarine on the surface and raced after his prize, using both submarine engines to go as fast as possible. The chase was on, with the *Amapala*'s captain sending updates to the U.S. Coast Guard and repeating that "a U-boat is pursuing us."

Knifing ahead at its maximum surface speed, U-507 closed the distance to the *Amapala*. When Schacht felt he was near enough, he had his gunner open fire with the smaller deck gun.

Captain Christiansen's pleas for help grew desperate: "Airplane, hurry up, I'm being shot at."

Schacht had his gunners move the light machine gun to the forward bridge. The commander recorded that U-507 "headed directly for the steamer," adding that the *Amapala* "received numerous hits on the bridge." Schacht was staying on the surface much too long; he knew that U.S. Navy aircraft would be closing in on him. But he gambled that in the "gloomy, rainy weather there is the hope that the aircraft will not find us." He was pushing his luck, almost the opposite of the way Würdemann used caution.

The sub continued to blast away with its machine gun.

Finally, with the ship's bridge full of bullet holes, Captain Christiansen stopped the engines so that he and his men could scramble into lifeboats.

Schacht wrote in his war diary that he ceased firing to allow the ship's crew to leave, and then he "maneuvered his boat abeam for a coup de grâce." He ordered his last torpedo fired, but it malfunctioned! The *Amapala* would apparently stay afloat and live to sail again.

Schacht, undaunted by the threat of U.S. aircraft arriving any minute, approached one of the lifeboats. After he demanded and received information about the ship from crewmen, the U-boat commander said he planned to send his sailors to open the hull valves on the still-floating ship so it would finally sink. Then he surprised *Amapala*'s crew in the life rafts by throwing them cigarette packs.

Schacht positioned the U-boat closer to the *Amapala*. He then ordered two of his men to swim to the ship and sink it by opening the sea cocks. The two submariners stripped down to their shorts, dived into the water, and climbed aboard the *Amapala*, going below to scuttle the ship. Minutes later, a U.S. bomber arrived on the scene. U-507 had to crash-dive, leaving the two German sailors stranded on the sinking ship!

The airplane dropped depth charges, shaking the sub but causing no serious damage. The Germans on the *Amapala*—who had found dry clothing and put it on—came running out on the deck to see what was happening. Somehow the pilots of the aircraft knew the enemy had boarded the ship, and they strafed the ship's deck with machine-gun fire. The outlook for those two German sailors was bleak. It appeared that their U-boat had fled, leaving them aboard an enemy vessel with no safe exit. Still, they followed their orders, opened the sea cocks, and abandoned ship in a life raft. Imagine their surprise when Schacht and U-507 surfaced nearby and hauled them inside!

Schacht recorded in detail how he brought his "commandos" back inside the sub. The two crewmen presented him with the papers of the steamer, among them the zigzag plan. The 4,148-ton steamer was owned by the Standard Fruit and Steamship Company, proceeding under the Honduras flag. Captain Christensen of the *Amapala* hollered to Schacht from his life raft that he did not know Germany was at war with Honduras or why his ship had been sunk. Schacht responded that the captain had ordered U.S. aircraft to bomb him. And on that exchange, Schacht finally decided he had pushed his luck far enough. The German commander set his sights on Lorient, writing, "A further stay at this location seemed unwise to me."

~

Erich Würdemann wasn't as reckless as Schacht (nor was he as colorful or detailed a writer in his war diary), but he was smart enough to stay in the vicinity of the Mississippi, knowing that without Schacht around he'd have prime pickings. He took full advantage of this situation and sank or severely damaged three tankers from May 14 to 17.

Since entering the Gulf, Würdemann had sunk or damaged seven ships, honed his hunting skills, and increased the body count. The first ship he attacked, the *Sama*, did not suffer any deaths, and the second, the *Aurora*, only one. But his last four attacks averaged 14 sailors killed per ship. So far on this mission, Würdemann's torpedoes had cost 70 sailors their lives—and, unlike Schacht, the young commander still had multiple torpedoes left.

With the section of ocean off the Mississippi buzzing with aircraft searching for the elusive subs, Würdemann could have moved to the less "hot" area off Texas or Alabama. But Dönitz had specifically wanted the young *Kapitänleutnant* to focus on the New Orleans area, and Würdemann decided he would stay for at least one more ship.

8

CLOSER TO HOME

Every day on the *Heredia* was a novel adventure for Sonny. The cook surprised him with new snacks, and he learned some of the crew's first names. Many of the sailors took time to explain the functions of various equipment. He and Lucille raced on the long, empty decks, even though Lucille always won. Sonny fared little better when he and Lucille played shuffleboard, and occasionally their dad joined in the competition. But the absence of other children on the boat meant that games with Lucille wore thin after a few days.

On his fourth day at sea, Sonny led the family to their lifeboat station for the daily drill. He and Lucille put on their own life jackets, but Ray insisted on tying the knot and pulling hard on it to make sure it held.

"I can do it myself, Dad," Sonny protested.

"I know you can, but my job is to make *sure* it's done right. In a real emergency, we only get one chance to tie it, and it has to stay put," his father said.

Sonny often found his father and mother talking in hushed tones on deck chairs, their books set aside. They spent long periods looking out at the horizon and didn't want to play checkers much. Sonny heard Ina say more than once that she wished the ship could go a lot faster. She looked uncomfortable and nervous, even when sitting outside under a blue sky.

Now the crewmen were polite but less interested in talking to Sonny and Lucille. There was a definite air of business and efficiency about them, much more so than in the early days of the voyage. Sonny tried to talk to the sailors who were looking out to sea with binoculars. He knew they were looking for subs. Sometimes he tried to help, but he found it boring after a moment or two.

Captain Colburn walked by and exchanged pleasantries with Ray, Ina, Lucille, and Sonny. He paused long enough to answer Sonny's questions, including why they had not seen more than one or two other ships. "Well, Sonny," said the captain, "it won't be long before we approach the shipping lanes outside New Orleans. There I expect you'll see your fair share of ships."

"Captain," Ray asked, "any new activity around here in the water?"

Colburn raised his eyebrows and turned a little to face the railing, perhaps hoping the children wouldn't be scared by what he had to say. "We get bulletins, Mr. Downs. We study them to ensure that the crew is aware of the latest safety precautions. But with submarines, yesterday's news doesn't matter much in today's waters, if you know what I mean."

"So they could be anywhere?" asked Ina.

"Yes, ma'am, Mrs. Downs. Anywhere," the captain answered.

"But we're through the worst part, aren't we?" Ray pressed the captain. "There should be antisub planes patrolling."

"Yes, Mr. Downs," the captain answered. "Every day brings us a little closer to complete safety. Until we're at the dock, we rely on these fine seamen to keep watch."

"And prayers to the Lord above," added Ina.

When the captain left, Sonny wanted to know more, but his dad just put one arm around him and the other around Ina. They looked out at the darkening sea.

"Two more days," Ina murmured. "Two more days and we'll be home safe."

~

That evening, May 16, the family elected not to sleep on the deck because the seas were building. The *Heredia* swayed from side to side in a stiffening wind. Ina worried that the kids might roll right off the deck chairs. Clouds had moved in, making a beautiful sunset but perhaps a rainy night. Better to be in their cabins below, where the ship's rocking would not be as pronounced.

Ina's decision was a good one. Several times she was awakened with a jolt during the night when a wave bigger than those that had preceded it rocked the *Heredia*. At dawn, the family climbed the mahogany stairs to the deck and were greeted by howling wind, driving rain, and waves cresting at 25 feet. The Downses huddled together and watched wind-whipped spray lash the ship while plumes of foam streaked by. The air temperature had dropped to 65 degrees, making them cold after their time in South America. Surprisingly, none of the family was seasick.

At breakfast the conversation was about how quickly the storm had a risen and the inaccuracy of weather forecasting. Part of the reason for the absence of a storm warning had to do with the war. Weather advisories had to be censored and cleared through the Weather Bureau Office in New Orleans, causing delays in the release of forecasts. In addition, the Weather Bureau relied on observation reports from ships scattered over hundreds of miles, but because of the presence of U-boats, the ships were under orders not to transmit radio messages, even about the weather. (In July of the following year, these factors caused a lack of preparedness when the "Surprise Hurricane of '43" careened into the Gulf, killing 19 people.)

Later that day, the lumbering waves subsided to 15 to 20 feet, but the ship still rolled heavily in the turbulent seas. From a passageway, Sonny and Ray watched whenever a crew member crossed the deck wearing a safety harness clipped to a cable. The *Heredia* sailors seemed right at home walking through the blasting wind and pelting rain.

Most of the U.S. Navy Armed Guardsmen aboard ships in 1942 were from 18 to 25 years old, and some were as young as 16. Many had enlisted in the navy wanting to serve aboard a fighting ship, such as a destroyer or an aircraft carrier, hoping to strike back at Japan for attacking Pearl Harbor. Instead, after boot camp, a handful were selected to serve aboard merchant ships—a less glamorous job in the minds of most. After a hasty three weeks of training to use the deck guns, the men were assigned to ships. While they may have longed for offensive action aboard destroyers, being in the Navy Armed Guard was by no means a safe or easy position. During World War II, 1,810 of these young men were killed or went missing.

~

"Can I go out on the deck, like the sailors?" asked Sonny. "I'll wear a harness."

Ray thought for a moment and surprised Sonny by saying, "If your mother says it's okay and I can find a sailor to go with you, I don't see why not."

Sonny didn't give his father a chance to change his mind. The boy raced below to find his mother.

Ina could see the excitement in Sonny's eyes as he described what he wanted to do. She knew the trip was near its end. Sonny would have a story he could tell over and over. "Let's go up to where your father is—I want to talk to him. If he thinks it is safe and you are right next to a sailor, I think it would be okay."

Sonny could not believe his good fortune. He grabbed his mother's hand, and together they joined Ray at the passageway. Ray had already recruited a sailor for the job. After they explained to Ina how safe it would be, she agreed.

The sailor fastened a harness on Sonny and then clipped him to the cable that ran to the bow of the ship. He did the same for himself. Together they stepped out into the driving rain and began slowly walking toward the bow.

Ina had second thoughts when she saw Sonny hunched over, struggling against the whipping wind and rain. She worried one strong gust might lift her boy into the air like a kite. But Sonny and the sailor safely reached the bow, and when they turned around, Sonny waved at her. Ina took a half step toward him, thinking that he was crying. Then she realized it was laughter coming from her son's mouth. He was having a ball. When he came back, Ina scooped him into her arms.

"Can I go again?" Sonny shouted, rubbing the burning salt spray from his eyes.

Ina laughed and shook her head. "Once is enough. You've got quite a story to tell Terry when you get home."

~

By the next day the air had become still and sticky. Around noon, a crew member reported seeing something unusual in the ocean, far off the stern. This caused quite a commotion, and the passengers and crew alike scanned the sea, wondering if the sighting could have been of a U-boat. The men of the Navy Armed Guard did the same, using their binoculars. Although there were no further sightings, Captain Colburn changed course for the closest harbor, which was Corpus Christi, Texas. Once there, the captain would go ashore for information, including whether the ship should stay in Corpus Christi Bay for the night.

Ina and Ray welcomed the change of course. Not only were they worried about the U-boat danger, but they were also ready to move on with the next phase of their life. Corpus Christi was closer to home than New Orleans was. They asked Captain Colburn if they could leave the ship there.

Upon reaching the outside of the bay, *Heredia*'s anchor was lowered. Captain Colburn was taken ashore in a pilot boat.

The entire Downs family stood at the rail and watched the captain leave, hoping he'd return with good news. They also noted that the bay was full of anchored ships. It was May 18, and they could actually see the shore of their home country for the first time in a year.

Ray was becoming edgy from sitting still, and Ina wanted to get off the ship. Sonny could hear his parents talking, already making plans for reuniting with Terry and searching for a place to live. Lucille, too, was ready to be back on land and to see her brother and grandparents. Only Sonny was sad to see the voyage come to an end. He was hoping for one last storm so he could go back out on deck with the harness and cable to enjoy the wind and plumes of spray.

Captain Colburn returned in an hour, climbing the Jacob's ladder back onto the boat and wearing a serious expression. The Downs family and a couple of other passengers waited expectantly by the rail.

"Sorry, folks," said the captain when he was on the deck. "They won't let you off here. There's too much paperwork and not enough time to get the necessary permission. But the officials say we should be fine steaming on toward New Orleans tonight." Then he surprised the passengers by passing out magazines and cigarettes to the adults and candy to the children.

"Was it a U-boat out there?" Ray asked. "Did the harbormaster tell you if others have seen it? Why are so many ships anchored in the bay?"

"Mr. Downs, due to wartime restrictions, including radio silence, there is little communication between ships and shore until a ship arrives in port," said the captain. He wore a stern expression and seemed exhausted by the trip ashore.

"I really want my family to get off the boat here, Captain," Ray said.

"We're uncomfortable going back out to sea," added Ina. "What about our children?"

"I'm terribly sorry," the captain said. "We cannot let you off here. Harbormaster's orders. I wish we could. I would not worry too much about something somebody might have seen hours ago. As I said before, if there's a submarine out there—and I said *if*—it could be anywhere. It's a big ocean, and there are a lot of boats in it. Chances are we'll be in New Orleans safely in no time."

"Looks like most of the boats are at anchor here, Captain," Ray pointed out, motioning toward the crowded bay. "They're safely in the harbor."

~

A half hour later, the *Heredia* was plowing east toward New Orleans. The magazines did little to lift Ina's mood. She watched the coast of Texas disappear with sadness.

A spectacular sunset with streaks of gold—the best of the voyage—briefly occupied Ina's attention. But after the sun dipped below the horizon and dusk darkened the ocean, she returned to brooding about U-boats. *If only we could have left the ship in Corpus Christi . . .*

That evening the captain ordered no lights be used on the *Heredia*. Small flashlights were allowed when passengers or sailors moved around. The Navy Armed Guards were at their lookout stations, enjoying the slight breeze but having difficulty seeing through a haze that hung over the ocean. Two of them were at the aft gun, two more in the forecastle, and a fifth on the bridge. The sixth serviceman was resting below.

The members of the Downs family were sitting together on deck chairs, quietly enjoying the cooler temperatures of the evening. They watched phosphorescence glimmer in the wake of the ship and talked in hushed voices. Sonny enjoyed the constant whooshing sound the ship made as it cut through the ocean. It looked like a beautiful moonlit night was in store.

A fellow passenger, Robert Beach, paced the deck nearby. Ina said, "Good evening, Mr. Beach."

Beach turned to Ina and gave a curt nod.

Ina saw the worried look on his face and said, "We'll be in port first thing in the morning."

"Not soon enough," said Beach as he walked away.

Sonny looked at his mother and asked, "Is he always so mean?"

Ina replied, "He's just anxious to get home. He's been in South America for three years." She didn't tell Sonny that Mr. Beach was especially nervous because he had spent a good deal of his income buying expensive jewelry in Panama. Beach was worried about not only his own welfare, but also the potential loss of his investment.

Sonny watched Mr. Beach scuttle away into the shadows. The boy switched subjects: "Can Lucille and I sleep on deck tonight?"

"Not tonight," answered Ray. "It's our last night. We've got to get our things organized, so we'll sleep in our staterooms."

Sonny knew better than to ask again, so he made a different request. "Because it's the last night, can you sleep in my room and Lucille can sleep with Mom?"

"Okay," said Ray.

"And can I sleep in my shorts, just like you?"

"Sure."

Sonny grinned, glad for one last night out of the ordinary.

A few minutes later, Captain Colburn, in his dress whites, strolled up and said good evening. The captain tousled Sonny's hair and said, "Well, young Downs, by six thirty in the morning we'll be docking in New Orleans."

"Yes, sir," said Sonny, "my dad told me. He and I are going to sleep in the same room for our last night."

Captain Colburn forced a smile. Ray stood up, and he and the captain moved out of earshot of the family. "Any more news about U-boats?" asked Ray.

"No, sir. We should be fine."

"How about news about the war?"

If the captain had gotten an update on the war and enemy action in the Gulf, he did not share it with the Downs family. Colburn shook his head. "Didn't have time to even ask when I was ashore. Guess we'll both learn more tomorrow morning when we are in New Orleans."

9

AN UNEASY FEELING

While Captain Colburn continued on his rounds, Ray wondered what was going on with the war. Several times during the voyage, he had asked the *Heredia's* radioman what he'd heard. The man's vague response was "nothing new."

In fact, a lot had happened during the week the Downs family was at sea. Much of the war news revolved around battles for oil fields abroad and the oil and gasoline shortages at home.

On the home front, U-boat attacks were interrupting the delivery of fuel, which was already in short supply due to military needs. Gasoline rationing began, and civilians were limited to three gallons of gasoline a week in many states. Despite this crisis, the New Orleans *Times-Picayune* reported that people were still unwilling to turn off outside lights at night, effectively helping U-boats find and sink ships.

Times-Picayune reports of ships torpedoed in the Gulf and the Caribbean Sea were becoming a daily occurrence. In fact, the Downses were quite lucky to have escaped unscathed when *Heredia* steamed through the Yucatán Channel, between the western end of Cuba and Mexico's Yucatán Peninsula. That was where a German U-boat sank seven ships in a two-week period, both before and after the *Heredia* somehow slipped through unharmed!

All the while, Ina and Ray were unaware of the toll U-boats were taking.

The *Heredia* had been lucky indeed, because defenses against U-boats in the Gulf of Mexico were even weaker than on the East Coast. By May 1942, ships on the East Coast were finally being protected by armed escorts; in the Gulf, however, ships were still traveling alone. There, the navy had only a couple of old destroyers, five cutters, an assortment of smaller craft, and 35 aircraft. That small force had difficulty finding a U-boat in the daytime in this nearly 618,000-square-mile area. It was almost impossible to locate one after sundown. Even when a U-boat was on the surface in daylight, inexperienced U.S. sailors and pilots sometimes overlooked it. U-boat crews were astounded when aircraft flew directly over them and nothing happened, or when patrol boats motored nearby without noticing the subs.

To compensate for the lack of armed ships to escort freighters, large civilian yachts were purchased by the military and converted to patrol boats. These vessels were equipped with depth charges and at least one .50-caliber machine gun. Coast Guard personnel usually operated these armed vessels, which rarely fought the enemy but were effective at patrolling and rescuing.

The navy and coast guard also reached out to commercial fishing vessels and civilian yacht clubs. Volunteers on small craft assisted the military with offshore observation; they would at least make it difficult for U-boats to surface and recharge their batteries. Even sailboat skippers volunteered, pointing out that sailors could climb the rigging to spot a U-boat or its periscope. The coast guard called them the "Corsair Fleet" and used them in the Coastal Picket Patrol, but the public called them the "Hooligan Navy."

Other experiments also held promise, such as using blimps to hover over merchant ships. The helium-filled blimps could cruise along at 50 miles an hour and watch over a wide swath of sea. They were armed with depth charges, but the airships were not easy to steer or quick to turn, making it difficult to get into position over a U-boat before it dived. The blimps' real value was in discouraging submarines from surfacing. Consolidated Aircraft's PBY Catalina flying boats were also used successfully as "protecting eyes" over merchant ships. Because they could land on and take off from the water, they were especially useful in search and rescue.

These various resources became increasingly effective in the second half of 1942. But in May 1942, when the *Heredia* was inching closer to safe port in New Orleans, effective defenses were limited. The first U-boat captains in the Gulf of Mexico, Schacht and Würdemann, enjoyed the element of surprise.

~

After Ray's conversation with Captain Colburn inquiring about the latest war news, the Downs family retired to their berths at 9:00 P.M. Sonny, thrilled to be sleeping with his father, climbed up to the top bunk while his father lay in the bottom bunk. Each of them checked that their life jackets—made of gray canvas covering balsa wood strands—were hanging on a peg within reach of their bunks. They talked for a couple of minutes, but soon both were fast asleep. In the next room, which was separated from Sonny's by the bathroom, Lucille had also fallen asleep, but not Ina. She simply could not shake a strong feeling of dread, and she tried in vain to let the ship's rocking calm her.

While Ina lay awake in her berth, the *Heredia* steamed eastward at 12 knots. She realized they had stopped zigzagging and were simply plowing into the night, and she hoped it was a good sign. Perhaps the captain had been told that evasive maneuvers were unnecessary because there were no submarines nearby. Still, she couldn't sleep.

The old ship was approximately 40 miles south-southwest of New Orleans, just a few miles from the Ship Shoal buoy.

~

While the Downs family spent their last afternoon and evening aboard the *Heredia*, Erich Würdemann maneuvered U-506 farther out into the Gulf and away from the Mississippi. He and his men had a dangerous job to perform: moving torpedoes from the deck down into the firing tubes. To do this, the U-boat had to remain on the surface, making it a target for any aircraft flying overhead. Using cables, a winch, pulleys, and considerable manpower, the crew wrestled the first 23-foot-long, 3,600-pound weapon from its deck housing and slowly lowered it on a rail through an open hatch into a torpedo tube. Then the process was repeated with the other deck torpedo as crewmen anxiously kept an eye on the sky, hoping no planes would appear.

Once the torpedoes were safely in their firing tubes, Würdemann ordered U-506 to submerge and set a course for the Ship Shoal buoy, which marked the entrance to the Mississippi River channel. The commander scanned the seas through the periscope. He spotted several fishing boats and one unloaded tanker that was so far away he declined to chase it. He knew that more ships would soon come along.

As darkness fell, Würdemann ordered the submarine back up to the surface and continued hunting, now just a few miles from the Ship Shoal buoy.

At approximately 1:00 A.M., Würdemann noted in his war diary that a shadow could be seen, meaning a ship was approaching. He changed course slightly so that his sub could lie in wait for it. Commander Würdemann knew that at night he could operate without the slightest risk of being detected. He'd be able to get so close to the ship that his torpedoes were almost guaranteed to find their mark.

PART II

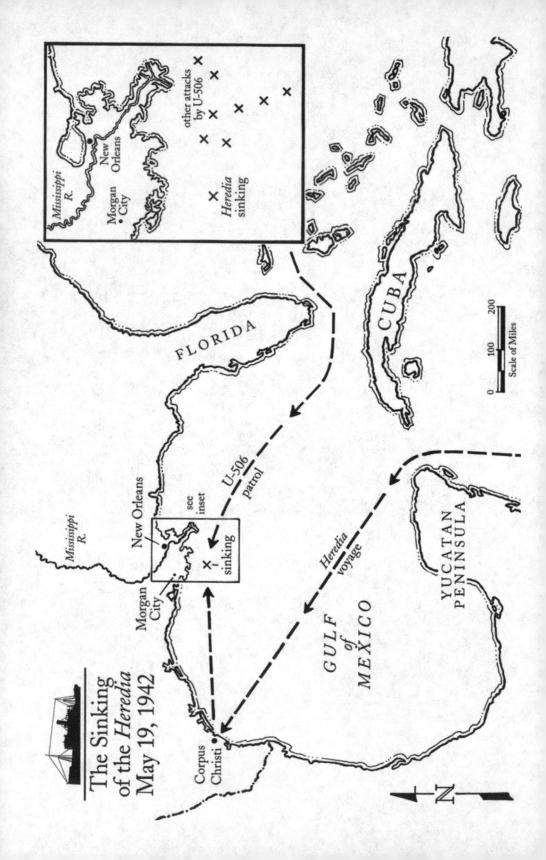

The Sinking of the *Heredia*
May 19, 1942

Mississippi R.

New Orleans

Morgan City

Corpus Christi

Heredia voyage

U-506 patrol

sinking

see inset

GULF of MEXICO

FLORIDA

CUBA

YUCATAN PENINSULA

Scale of Miles

0   100   200

N

Inset:

Mississippi R.

New Orleans

Morgan City

other attacks by U-506

Heredia sinking

10

TORPEDOES IN THE NIGHT

The first torpedo tore into the *Heredia* with a tremendous explosion, causing the old ship to shudder. Sonny struggled to sit up in the top bunk of the cramped, dark cabin. *Did we hit the pier in New Orleans?*

Then, *BOOM!* The second torpedo rocked the boat so hard that Sonny almost fell to the floor.

Ray turned on the cabin light and it flickered, casting an eerie glow on his ashen face. He was now standing next to the bunk bed.

Sonny felt his father's hands on his shoulders.

"Put on your life preserver," Ray barked. "Tie it tight and stay right here."

Confused and afraid, Sonny could see water sloshing around his father's ankles as his dad opened the door to his mother's cabin.

Snatching his life jacket from the peg next to his bunk, Sonny fumbled with the straps. The life jacket's bulk pushed awkwardly against his ears as he pulled the ties together across his chest. *Is Dad coming back?* Sonny wondered, his fear growing as more water swirled into the cabin. *The ship must be sinking!* He could hear shouting in the hallway. He considered hopping off the bunk and running for the lifeboats, as he had been taught to do.

He was about to holler for his father when Ray burst back into the room. He was followed by Ina and Lucille. Lucille's life vest was secured over her nightclothes, while Ina, her face stricken, had grabbed a coat to put over her nightgown, and secured a life vest over it.

Ray lifted Sonny off the top bunk and tugged at his son's life jacket to be sure it was secure. "You did a good job. Now, hold my hand and don't let go!"

The family left the cabin and entered the corridor, hand in hand. Pale blue lights lining the passageway flickered. They saw Mr. Beach just outside his cabin door, but he was going back inside rather than going to the lifeboat station. Ray shouted, "What are you doing? Head up on deck!"

"Got to get my suitcases!" shouted Mr. Beach. Just as he ducked inside his cabin, the lights went out for good.

Sonny felt like everything was in slow motion. His father

gripped his fingers so tightly it hurt. But knowing his dad was there helped Sonny feel less scared.

At the end of the corridor a sailor swung two flashlights in wide arcs. The family sloshed that way, the water now up to Sonny's thighs.

"Don't come down here! Take the stairs to the deck!" the sailor shouted. "We've been torpedoed!"

Sonny was confused: This was not the usual route to their lifeboat station. And how did the ship get torpedoed with those guards standing watch? But he focused on keeping up with his dad's long strides.

Hurrying up the steps, Sonny saw a bit of light coming from the deck above. It seemed to take forever to climb those stairs and escape the rushing water below. People were shouting on deck, and Sonny wondered if the *Heredia* might be on fire.

Just as the family reached the top of the steps, more disaster struck.

The ship suddenly lurched to starboard, and they were slammed by an avalanche of churning water. Sonny's hand was torn from his father's grasp. The boy felt himself tumbling underwater as if inside a washing machine, not sure which way the surface was. He opened his eyes but saw only blackness, which added to his confusion and fear. Someone grabbed one of his legs and he kicked away. His lungs ached for air as he thrashed wildly. He clawed at the water, panicked that the ocean would never let him go.

Ten seconds later, his head broke the surface. Sonny came up gasping for air, then coughed up seawater. He swiveled around, desperately looking for his parents and sister. They were gone. He was alone in the ocean alongside the ship, terrified.

Sonny tried to scream, but a wave slapped him in the face, and he swallowed more seawater.

Now he wondered if he was dreaming, because it was so bright around him that he thought it was daylight. *Am I dead? Is this a nightmare?* The eight-year-old didn't know that the brilliant light came from a powerful searchlight on the conning tower of U-506.

Sonny tried to make sense of what he could see. He knew he was in the ocean—could feel the swells rising and falling—but he also heard voices coming from somewhere above him. He looked toward the sound and saw what he thought was the center of the *Heredia*, the uppermost deck above the bridge, where the machine guns were mounted. But everything was at a crazy angle, and it took him a moment to process it. Then he understood: the ship was tilted to starboard, and the entire stern was underwater. The rest of the ship stuck out of the ocean at a 45-degree angle.

In an incredible stroke of luck, Sonny surfaced just a few feet from a short steel ladder leading to the upper deck. He swam to it and tried to climb its five or six steps.

Sonny only managed to scale a couple of steps before sliding back down. The angle of the ship made climbing the ladder almost impossible. Holding on to the ladder, the boy shouted for help, but only a faint croak came from his mouth. *Where's Dad? I need him now!*

Again the boy attempted to ascend the ladder, and this time when he fell off, he landed right on top of a man. His silent prayer was answered, but it wasn't Ray who came to the rescue. The thin, gawky, balding man whom Sonny fell against was George Conyea, a fellow passenger from New Orleans.

"We gotta get up there!" shouted Conyea. "You try again, and I'll be right behind you!"

This time the boy made it to the top, with Conyea right behind him.

"You stand by the wire rail," Conyea shouted, "and hold on to it!"

Sonny could only nod; too much was happening, and he was shaking from a combination of cold, exhaustion, and fear.

Conyea pointed to the wire cable supported by posts that encircled the upper deck. That's when Sonny realized there was another man standing on the top deck: Captain Erwin Colburn. The captain, still wearing his white uniform, was struggling to free a life raft from its brackets. Binoculars dangled from his neck as he cursed at the stubborn raft.

"Where's my family?" Sonny shouted. Silence. Neither Conyea nor the captain said a word, nor did they even meet Sonny's eyes. It was a crushing blow for the boy. He choked back a sob, thinking his mother, father, and Lucille had all been swallowed by the ocean.

Both Conyea and the captain stooped and resumed pulling on the raft, even kicking at the brackets that held it in place.

Searching for any sign of his family, Sonny looked down at the black five-foot swells sliding beneath the ship. From the vantage point of the upper deck, the boy now realized just how desperate his situation was. The entire stern of the ship was submerged. The radio shack and lifeboats had been destroyed, and jagged pieces of metal protruded from the lower deck just behind where he stood. It looked as if the *Heredia* would break into two pieces at any minute.

Sonny also saw the source of the light. About 200 yards away, the searchlight from the sub cut through the darkness, seeming to point directly at the boy. He wasn't sure what the sub might do next, but Sonny was thankful for the light, as it allowed him to continue scanning the ocean's surface for any signs of his family. Although he could hear distant shouts for help, he couldn't see anyone, nor did the shouts sound like members of his family. *Are these two men and I the only ones left on the ship?* He shivered in the cool night air. His only clothing was his wet shorts, and he felt colder now than he had in the water.

Sonny watched Conyea and Captain Colburn move to the same side of the raft and pull together, still without result. The raft was small, just a simple four-foot-by-four-foot balsa wood frame. Gray canvas was wrapped around the balsa wood but did not cover the middle. It reminded Sonny of a sandbox with no bottom. He realized that even if they got it free, it would not be like sitting in a boat, as they would have only the frame to hold on to. But no raft at all meant a death sentence, and even the eight-year-old boy knew that—the ocean was clearly pulling the ship down. More of the ship was underwater now than had been just a minute earlier, when Sonny had first reached the gun deck.

Still clutching the wire cable, Sonny noticed movement where the ocean covered the submerged part of the ship on the starboard side. A man burst from the water and swam toward him. The man was his father!

~

Commander Erich Würdemann stood on the bridge with some of his men and quietly watched the stricken *Heredia* wallowing in the water. He would have preferred sinking an oil tanker rather than a merchant ship. Still, he was satisfied that the *Heredia* was another kill, adding to his tonnage, just as Admiral Dönitz had instructed. Würdemann did not want to use another torpedo, so he waited to make sure the *Heredia* went to the bottom of the sea. If needed, he'd use his guns to put holes near the waterline of the vessel and speed the process.

The commander watched small figures moving on the ship's uppermost deck, where machine guns were mounted, but he was unconcerned. The bow section of the ship extended from the sea at such a steep angle that he surmised the guns would be useless. He was also unconcerned about aircraft. Even if the radio operator had sent out an SOS, it would take an aircraft at least a half hour to arrive on the scene. If an airplane appeared, the U-boat commander would simply shut off his light and move away. And if another ship came to pick up survivors, he'd submerge to periscope depth and torpedo that ship as well. Efficiency was what Dönitz's training was all about, and Würdemann lived it.

The German U-boat commander watched the men on the upper deck of the ship struggling with what was probably the life raft. He could see a child standing behind them. Someone else was in the water, swimming toward the group on the deck. Unlike the U-507 commander, Schacht, Erich Würdemann had no plans to talk to any survivors to learn more about the ship or to wish them luck. He could estimate the tonnage of the ship, and now all he really cared about was seeing it sink with his own eyes. But if the group on the ship's upper deck did not leave the vessel soon, he might fire a warning shot to indicate that they'd best get in the water immediately. It was ships he was after, not human lives. While death was a casualty of ships being torpedoed, the Germans did not shoot those who had survived.

11

INA, LUCILLE,
AND A SINKING SHIP

INA

When the Downs family was escaping from the lower deck of the *Heredia* and the ship lurched, rushing water tore Lucille from her mother's grip. Ina heard Lucille scream, "Mother, where are you?" Then the young mother found herself underwater, tumbling in the churning ocean, more terrified than she had ever been in her life.

An eddy of water pinned Ina against a wall, beneath a ladder to an upper deck. As the swirling black sea rose, Ina felt helpless. She was trapped, unable to move and unsure where her children and husband were. Then in a split second the eddy shifted and pushed her upward. She was able to grab on to a window and perch on the sill, looking out toward the sea as the ship groaned and shuddered beneath her. She glanced around for her family but saw no one. Self-preservation kicked in, and she heard a voice in her head say, *Jump or you'll go down with the ship.*

She pushed away from the ship, feeling her stomach in her throat. She fell through the air and into the water.

When Ina's head broke the surface, she felt herself covered in a warm gooey substance. It was oil from the ship's engines that was spreading from the sinking vessel. Gasping for air, she looked around frantically for her family, desperate for Ray and the children. She tried to clear her vision with an oil-soaked hand. There was no one around, and the only source of light was on the other side of the ship. She didn't know what it was or how she'd reach it.

She attempted to call out for help but could only manage a gasp. The acrid smell of oil stung her throat, and panic squeezed her airway to a sliver. Oil was in her eyes, limiting her sight, but she was well aware that she was utterly alone, drifting away from the ship.

Just minutes before, Ina had been safe with her family. Now she felt like she was in a nightmare. But it was all too real. She remembered the sequence of events that had resulted in her being here, in the oily water at night.

Before going to bed, she'd lingered over trimming her fingernails and brushing her hair, not knowing why except that it was to be her family's last night on board. Later, unable to sleep, she'd thought about her family's future. She had faith that, with Ray's mechanical skills, they could settle back into a productive life in

Texas. Then her quiet, pensive night had been blown apart with the blast that threw Lucille out of her bunk, catapulting Ina into action.

"Oh, Mother, was that a torpedo?" Lucille cried out. Without a thought, Ina grabbed their life jackets from under the lower bunk. The lights flickered, but she still had the presence of mind to knot the ties of the life jackets firmly.

She couldn't remember exactly what had happened next. One minute she had been climbing the mahogany stairs, holding Lucille's hand, and the next minute she was tumbling alone in a river of seawater cascading over the deck.

Where is Lucille now? Ina thought, and her tears mixed with the ocean surrounding her.

~

LUCILLE

When the ship suddenly lurched as the family reached the top of the stairs, Lucille found herself trapped by a seething whirlpool on a lower deck. The water around her boiled and swirled. Terrible noises were coming from the structure that had seemed so solid and indestructible just hours before. Though she was a strong, independent girl, being torn from her family in the darkness shocked her to her core, leaving a frightened, panicked child screaming for her mother. She was flailing around, unsure what to do next, when a voice called out to her from above.

"Lucille, I'm coming to help you," said a man. He quickly

descended a ladder from a steeply sloped upper deck that was pointing toward the sky. Then he let go and jumped into the water next to her. She recognized him as one of the friendly sailors who had doted on her and Sonny throughout the trip. He spoke with a curious accent that wasn't Spanish and wasn't anything she'd heard in Texas. His name was Roy, she remembered. He was the second mate on the *Heredia*, a tall, tan, and handsome man, Roy Sorli.

"Come with me," he said. "We can't stay in here; we need to get outside the ship."

"But my mother and dad—I need to find them and Sonny," she pleaded.

"Yes, we will," he answered. "First we need to climb back up there where I was and jump off the other side into the ocean. We need to get away from the ship; it's going to sink. I'm sure your parents are outside in one of the life rafts. They must be looking for you."

He pulled her from the swirling water and pushed her toward the ladder he had descended. When they reached the top, he boosted Lucille up to the edge of the listing hull. The steel beneath her feet was vibrating with the horrific noises of explosions as bulkheads blew and water rushed into every available space. Just as Sorli climbed to the edge, another sailor's head popped out of a porthole.

"Sorli, is that you?" the man asked as he looked around.

"Robello, you need to get out of there before the ship goes down!" Sorli shouted. "We're about to jump."

"I know, I was trying the door—I thought she was going to roll over," the sailor responded. "I think I can get out this way."

The sailor wiggled one shoulder, then the other, through the tiny porthole, pushing up with his hands until his whole naked body slipped out. Soon he was next to them, his skin glowing in the glare of the searchlight from the U-boat. Sorli took off his jacket and handed it to the sailor, providing the naked man with a shred of protection against the sea.

They stepped to the edge of the hull, where there was nothing but darkness beyond. Sorli grabbed Lucille's quivering hand. "We jump on three and swim as fast as we can away from the boat," he said.

Lucille looked down at the water, terrified of leaping into the abyss. But she had to put her trust in this man until her parents found her. "I'm ready," she said softly.

"One, two, three!" Sorli hollered, and together they were falling through the humid air, toward an unknown fate.

Lucille hit the water with a smack, and her life vest rose up and covered her face. She frantically pulled it back into place. The first thing she saw was the sagging hulk of the *Heredia*, still illuminated by the U-boat searchlight.

Sorli tugged on her arm. "Keep your head down and swim," said Sorli. "We have to swim fast."

There was no time to ask the questions that nagged at Lucille. *Where are the lifeboats? When will I find Mother and Dad? How long will we be in the water?*

"Swim, Lucille, don't stop. We need to be far from the ship

when it goes down," he said. "You're a brave girl and a good swimmer. Keep swimming."

Just then a louder explosion sent shock waves through the water, and the stern of the ship completely disappeared beneath the waves. The water swirled around Lucille, tugging at her pajamas. The hissing and spitting of the sinking ship sounded like an angry dragon ready to devour her. She swam as hard as she could, trying to keep up with Sorli and Robello.

There was another man swimming nearby, third mate Thomas Burke, who joined the small band escaping the wreck.

"Keep going," said Sorli.

"No time to stop now," added the other sailor.

"I'm trying," said Lucille.

"Then why do you keep stopping?" Sorli asked.

"Because my pajamas are falling down," said Lucille, yanking up her waterlogged pajama pants.

Burke snorted. "Okay, can't help that," he said. "I think we're just about out of danger, but we should keep swimming to get clear of the debris and oil."

Lucille had taken swimming lessons in South America and knew how to kick and paddle with her arms, so she kept at it, remembering her mother's glowing approval when she'd advanced a level. That warm, sunny place seemed so foreign and far away now.

The 11-year-old felt tears and panic welling up with the memory of her mother smiling when Lucille and Sonny demonstrated the swimming strokes they'd learned. But swimming in a Costa Rican lagoon was far different from putting the skills to the test in the open ocean. Waves slapped her face, debris from the wreck got in her way, and there were no sandy beach and dry towel waiting for her. She tried to breathe steadily and stay close to Roy Sorli.

Human noises could be heard in the darkness, vague groans and men hollering. But there were no voices Lucille recognized. *My parents must be looking for me*, she thought, *but why can't I hear them calling?*

12

THE RAFT

SONNY AND RAY

Sonny could not believe his eyes. It was as if his father had risen from the dead, the way he'd burst from the water.

When the boat initially lurched and the family became separated, the avalanche of water pushed Ray back down the staircase and washed him around like a matchstick. Several times he found air pockets, only to be pulled back under the swirling water. Somehow, by swimming and being pushed by the water, Ray found himself in the flooded galley. He hollered for Sonny, Ina, and Lucille, but no one answered.

Ray repeatedly dived down into the black water, frantically groping around. He was feeling for a body in case one of his family members had also been washed into the room and was trapped. *Where are they?* They could be on the outside of the ship in the ocean. They could have been flushed to the bottom of the mahogany staircase and unable to get back up. The ship was making terrible groaning noises from metal being twisted by intense water pressure, and there were loud hissing sounds from escaping air. Time was running out. Ray was afraid the *Heredia* would plunge to the seabed at any moment.

Seeing light coming from a window, he swam to it and used his feet to break the glass, slashing his right leg just above the knee.

Ray swam through the glass and kicked to the surface, and the first thing he saw was the tiny upper gun deck illuminated by a bright light. He was confused, but he didn't waste any time, immediately swimming to the deck and scrambling aboard. The first word he heard was "Dad!"

Ray hugged his son and then assessed the situation, noting that the captain and Conyea were the only other people on the deck. The U-boat was just 200 yards away, off the stern. Ray thought the Germans might open fire with their machine guns at any second. He turned to the captain and Conyea.

"What the heck is the matter with you guys? We gotta get off this ship!"

Captain Colburn responded, "We can't get the raft out of the mounts."

Ray pushed the captain aside, yelling, "You jackasses!" Next, he took a quick look at the way the raft was mounted. He squatted, putting both hands under one side of the balsa wood, and in a single quick motion wrenched it free of the brackets.

Ray turned back to the captain. "I'm going to have Sonny lie on top of one side of the raft, and while he's holding on, I'll slide it into the water. Then we'll jump in the water and swim to it."

"I need to be on it when you slide it off!" shouted the captain.

"Why?"

"I can't swim," Colburn responded.

Ray jabbed a fist into the captain's chest, roaring, "Well, you're going to learn real quick, because my son goes first!"

Sonny, watching this exchange, was as stunned as Colburn. He had viewed the captain as the ultimate authority, like a school principal. Now, however, there had been a clear shift in who was in charge, and Sonny sensed that the change was permanent. He knew what his father was like when he was riled and in a hurry.

Ray felt a sense of urgency beyond the threat of the ship sinking, beyond the possibility of the U-boat's machine guns firing at them, and even beyond the chance of the ship's boiler exploding and blowing the *Heredia* to smithereens. He wanted to get that raft in the water immediately and start searching for his wife and daughter. His bleeding knee throbbed, but he ignored it and stepped toward the raft.

"Get out of the way!" Ray shouted at the captain.

Colburn moved aside.

Ray positioned the raft at the aft section of the deck, where the drop to the water would be only about four feet. Then he lifted Sonny and put him on top, saying "Just hold on tight. As soon as I slide you down, I'm jumping off, and I'll climb on the raft right next to you. We're going to be all right."

Sonny hugged one side of the hollow square, his fingers digging into the canvas. Terrified of going back down into the dark ocean, he closed his eyes. Then he felt his father slide the raft a foot or two and shove it over the side.

The raft splashed into the water with a jolt, and Sonny lost his grip but managed to stay onboard. He lifted his head and saw his father, Conyea, and the captain leap off the deck and into the sea. They landed just a couple of feet away amid floating debris. The three men scrambled aboard, and Ray immediately lay on top of Sonny, trying to protect the boy, worried that the Germans might strafe them with bullets from their machine guns. The three adults used their hands to begin paddling the raft away from the crippled ship.

Ray's weight was pushing Sonny so low that he swallowed seawater and tried to squirm out from under his father, his lungs screaming for air.

~

U-BOAT COMMANDER WÜRDEMANN

Commander Würdemann watched the boy and the men escape the ship, but he kept his searchlight on the *Heredia*. He stayed nearby to make sure the vessel sank.

Würdemann and the other Germans on the conning tower

were amazed that part of the *Heredia* was still floating after taking multiple torpedoes to its hull. He could hear people shouting for help in the water, but that was of no concern to him. The commander kept his searchlight on the stricken ship, thinking the time had come to blast it with his deck gun. He watched the men on the raft furiously paddling and kicking away with their arms and legs. The commander decided to give the ship a little more time before he put an artillery shell into its hull.

Würdemann stood by the *Heredia* for a few more minutes and then saw what he'd been waiting for. The bow of the ship finally gave up the fight and followed the stern into the sea. The commander later recorded the following in his war diary: "Steamer settles astern quickly. Initially the foreship protrudes up to the bridge, later however that sinks also . . . Accepted size: 5,200 gross registered tons."

Würdemann ordered the sub to move away, to see if he could find and sink another ship in the same night.

~

Ray's fear that the U-boat would strafe them with the machine gun was unfounded. Throughout World War II, there was only one documented case of a German U-boat commander ordering his men to open fire on survivors in the water or on life rafts. In the hundreds of other sinkings by U-boats, there was not a single case or accusation of this kind of behavior. In fact, just two days before the *Heredia* attack, a U-boat commander had gone out of his

way to help a survivor: a sailor with a shattered elbow was struggling to stay afloat in the ocean after his ship was torpedoed. He
was unable to reach a life raft on which other survivors had found
refuge. The U-boat commander saw his plight and "scooped him
up with the bow" of his submarine. Then, in broken English, the
commander called to the life raft to "come on over and get this
man." After the men on the life raft picked up the injured man,
one shouted to the U-boat commander that they wanted cigarettes. The commander threw over two packs and said, referring
to the attack, "You can thank Mr. Roosevelt for this, I am sorry."

German U-boat men, from Dönitz all the way down to the
lowest-ranking sailor, had a code of conduct that did not allow
the killing of survivors in the water. However, in the Pacific, it
was a very different scenario. Japanese submarine commanders
routinely tried to kill anyone who didn't go down with the ship.

On the night of July 2, 1944, Japanese submarine I-8, commanded by Tatsunosuke Ariizumi, sent two torpedoes into the
U.S. ship *Jean Nicolet* in the Pacific. All of the crew and passengers
on the *Jean Nicolet* were able to safely abandon the sinking ship
and board life rafts and lifeboats. A Japanese sailor ordered the
survivors onto the bow of I-8, where they were brutally attacked.
When the sub crash-dived to avoid an approaching aircraft, the
injured were washed into the sea, many with their hands tied. Of
the 100 men who evacuated the sinking ship, 24 survived.

13

A MOST HOPELESS NIGHT

SONNY AND RAY (FIRST HOUR IN THE OCEAN)

The raft's square shape didn't help, but Ray, Conyea, and the captain were able to get some distance from the sinking ship. At any minute they expected disaster to strike from an explosion of the *Heredia*'s boiler, or a whirlpool of suction if the ship suddenly went down. Bits of debris floated all around them, but they saw no other survivors.

Sonny had managed to squirm out from under his father, and he was now in the middle of the raft. His arms clutched the raft's edge and his legs dangled in the ocean. The three adults were in similar positions, either on the middle or outside edge of the raft.

Conyea started to say something, but Ray suddenly yelled, "I can hear Ina shouting! I'm going back!"

"You can't go back," hollered Captain Colburn. "You'll never make it!"

Conyea, too, shouted at Ray. "The ship is going to sink any minute! The sub is still there. I can see its light!"

"I don't care," boomed Ray. "I heard Ina!"

"You can't be sure it was her!" pleaded the captain.

Sonny was terrified that his father would leave him and never make it back. He watched in fear as his dad moved from the middle of the raft to the outer edge. Conyea positioned himself next to Ray, grabbing Ray's life jacket. "Your son needs you here!"

Ray swatted Conyea's arm away, then looked back at Sonny. He was torn between keeping his son alive and making a dash for the voice that he was sure was Ina's.

"Let's listen," reasoned Captain Colburn, "and see if we hear another shout."

Ray moved back toward Sonny.

The four survivors didn't speak as the raft drifted farther from the death throes of the *Heredia*. The vessel continued to emit loud bubbling and gurgling noises as it settled lower in the water.

Finally, the captain broke the silence. "The sub has moved off. I can't see its light."

"Can anyone see the ship?" asked Conyea.

Without the light from the sub, none of the survivors could see the vessel, nor could they hear the noises it had made just minutes earlier. Ray tried to put Ina out of his mind and focus on saving his son.

"We can sit on the edge of the raft," said Ray to the others, "but we gotta spread out."

Conyea took two strokes and perched on the edge opposite Ray. The captain, his face in a tense grimace because he didn't know how to swim, slowly inched to the side just to the right of Ray and carefully pulled himself up. Sonny went to the side of the square to the left of his father. The boy pulled himself up and into a sitting position. Because Sonny weighed only a third as much as each of the other men, his side of the raft rose out of the water, while the captain's end was so low that the water almost reached his neck.

"This won't do!" bellowed Ray. "One wave and we're going over. Mr. Conyea, you and I gotta scoot over closer to Sonny's side."

This simple move helped balance the raft. However, the weight of the three men plus Sonny was enough to submerge the raft a few inches, so that from the waist down their bodies were underwater. It was a delicate balancing act, but at least their upper torsos were relatively dry, which would help ward off hypothermia.

Ray glanced at Sonny, worried that the boy would be the first victim of the cold ocean because of his small size.

"Are you cold, son?"

"I'm okay, Dad."

"Well, if you get really cold, just tell me, and you can sit on my lap and I'll wrap my arms around you."

The air temperature was in the upper 60s and the water temperature about 75 degrees. The relatively warm temperature of the ocean might not seem dangerous, but it was far short of the normal 98.6-degree body temperature. Making matters worse, cold water draws off a person's heat about 25 times faster than air does at the same temperature. If Sonny's core temperature dropped to 95 degrees, he'd start shivering. Soon his extremities would start to feel numb as the blood vessels constricted. That is the body's way of decreasing heat loss through the skin and keeping blood flowing to the vital organs. Layers of fat would also slow the cooling of the blood, but eight-year-old Sonny was as thin as a sapling.

~

INA (First Hour in the Ocean)

Ina, too, was chilled by the unforgiving ocean. She floated near the ship and could hear horrifying sounds of people screaming and the vessel breaking apart. A broken board bumped into her and she grabbed it, leaning forward and kicking her feet to propel herself away from the ship, the destruction and carnage.

She and her family had been told countless times during lifeboat drills that a sinking ship creates tremendous suction and whirlpools that might drown anyone nearby, but now it was real. As she fought to put distance between herself and the doomed *Heredia*, the water around her boiled with bubbles, and debris popped up to the surface.

She found her voice. "Raymond! Sonny! Lucille!" she screamed again and again, knowing it would be a miracle for her shouts to carry above the cries of the injured and the awful noises of the ship being torn apart by the sea. Her mind was wild with thoughts of losing her children. If only she had held tighter to Lucille. The girl's last plea for her mother haunted Ina's thoughts.

When she stopped for a breath, she felt small fish bumping against her legs, sending Ina into a frenzy of kicking to keep them at bay. Being alone in the water in the darkness of the night, coupled with the thought of predatory fish, tempted panic. Ina was traumatized. Fortunately, she could hear other voices from time to time, men's voices, so she knew that others were nearby. She hoped a rescue ship would be arriving quickly. And she prayed that both Lucille and Sonny were with Ray.

~

LUCILLE (FIRST TWO HOURS IN THE OCEAN)

"Where are the life rafts?" Lucille asked Sorli. "I can't swim much longer."

"We'll take care of you," Sorli said. He grabbed a wooden box that was bobbing nearby. "We might be able to use this." Then he popped the lid open and pulled out a long string of colorful flags. Lucille recognized them as the signal flags that had fluttered high up on the *Heredia*'s yardarms just the day before, when the ship arrived in Corpus Christi. They were a stark contrast to the black water all around, but she couldn't imagine what they'd do with flags. Perhaps wave them at a passing ship?

Sorli grabbed a hatch cover that was floating nearby, and then a piece of wood. Burke helped him lash the flotsam together with the flags. "Okay, Lucille, climb up here," Sorli said, helping her onto the makeshift raft. The sailors hung on to the edges to stay afloat, sometimes talking softly to each other and looking down into the dark water below.

Lucille looked back at where she thought the ship had been, but it was now dark in all directions.

"Who's that?" called a voice nearby.

"Sorli, Burke, and Robello, and one civilian!" Sorli answered.

A man hanging on to a board appeared from the gloom—another member of the crew. "Any idea how many made it out?" he asked. Nobody answered.

Sorli had been on watch when the first torpedo hit, and he knew the ship was just a few miles from the Ship Shoal buoy. He worried that the current of the nearby Mississippi River would push the survivors far into the Gulf by the time rescue planes were sent out. He estimated that by midmorning the New Orleans harbormaster would alert the navy that the *Heredia* was overdue. Because they were subject to radio silence, the harbormaster might hesitate to send search parties out immediately, giving the ship a buffer of time to reach its destination. If that were true, rescue planes might not launch until afternoon. And it could take the searchers more than 24 hours to find them. Sorli wondered if any of them would still be alive.

Two torpedoes had ripped through the hull of the *Heredia*, ensuring that there was no time to send distress signals. Those same torpedoes blew apart the life rafts. The survivors would have to rely on the flotsam from the wreck to keep their heads above water until help arrived.

Burke, at 23, was among the youngest of the sailors in the group, a recent Massachusetts Maritime Academy graduate who knew the code of the sea. Sailors always rendered help to others, but war was upending everything he knew. These U-boats were sinking anything they came upon, whether an oil tanker or a merchant ship. Burke hoped the Germans had spared the shrimp boats that plied the Gulf, knowing those were their best chance of rescue—if their paths crossed.

Lucille began to cry quietly, the shock and separation from her family starting to set in.

"Now, Lucille, you'll have a lot to tell your mother and dad when they find us," Sorli said to comfort her. "Have you ever swum in the ocean before? Have you ever built a raft like Robinson Crusoe? This is quite an adventure for you."

"I did swim in the ocean, in Costa Rica," she said. "There were big waves at the beach, and Sonny got knocked over by one."

"That's funny," said Sorli. "Now, you're from Texas. Have you ever seen snow? I'm from a place with a lot of snow."

"No, but I want to," she said. "Did you build snowmen? I've seen pictures of them."

The chatter helped distract Lucille from her worries, but even she thought it peculiar to be in the ocean in the middle of the night talking about snowmen. She knew Sorli was trying to console her, and she didn't resist.

"Yes, snowmen," Sorli said. "We had so much snow in Norway that I would ski to school. Have you seen skiing?"

Lucille shook her head.

Burke spoke up: "It's like ice-skating, except you don't have to be on a pond. Skis are long boards on your feet that let you slide over the snow. I'm from a place that gets a lot of snow, too. Boston."

"I would surely like to try that," said Lucille. "Sonny got a scooter for Christmas, and he wants to ride it to school when we go back to San Antonio. Will someone be able to get it out of the ship when we get rescued? And my dad's car—it was on the ship, too."

The talk ebbed and flowed, with Sorli doing his best to keep Lucille's spirits up and direct her thoughts away from her family, the plight they were all in, and the cold they all felt right to their bones.

About two hours had gone by since the *Heredia* had been torpedoed, and Lucille shivered as she sat on the hatch cover and boards with her legs dangling in the water. The men were talking among themselves, but she was so tired and cold that she didn't listen.

She forced herself to stay awake, afraid of falling off the hatch cover. Amusing herself by splashing a bit of water with her foot, she was fascinated by the phosphorescence that spattered on the surface like a glowing sparkler. Pieces of the makeshift raft knocked together in the trough of each small wave that briefly lifted it, and that, too, helped her stay awake. The thought of sharks caused a new kind of chill to shoot through her body. She considered asking Mr. Sorli about the possibility of sharks, but she didn't even want to say the word out loud. It was so frightening to consider, she forced herself to focus on listening to the men talk. Anything to keep her mind off what might lurk below.

14

BATTLING THE COLD

SONNY AND RAY

(SECOND AND THIRD HOURS IN THE OCEAN)

Ray vowed to himself that he'd do whatever it took to keep his son warm, even if it meant hoisting Sonny out of the water and somehow putting the boy on his shoulders.

In the darkness, the father could faintly see Sonny's shape but not the features of his face because high, thin clouds blocked out most of the light from the stars and moon. Ray looked toward Sonny and thought, *This is all my fault. I should have known the full danger when they made me sign the release papers before we boarded the ship.* He shook his head, realizing that this kind of thinking was torture. *Stop. Just focus on Sonny.*

A minute later, Sonny, as if reading his father's thoughts, asked, "Will Mom and Lucille be all right?"

"They should be fine," lied Ray. "They are probably floating on a raft just like us."

"That's right," said Captain Colburn. "The ship had three rafts."

"Where were we when the ship was torpedoed? How far from port?" Conyea asked the captain.

"About forty miles out from New Orleans. To the southwest."

Ray turned his head in the direction of the captain and asked, "When do you think help will come?"

Captain Colburn hesitated before answering, concerned about saying anything negative in front of Sonny.

"Just tell us the truth," said Ray. "We're going to be fine no matter how long we have to sit on this raft."

"Okay," said Colburn. "We were operating on radio silence, but that doesn't really matter, because I think the section of the ship where the radio was took a direct hit from one of the torpedoes. So the authorities on shore only know that we were scheduled to reach New Orleans about six A.M. I'm guessing that by eight A.M. they will become concerned. One of the patrol planes will start looking for us."

Conyea, who was from New Orleans, added, "And we might get lucky. There are probably several Coast Guard and shrimp boats in the area, and one of them may find us at dawn."

"You're right, Mr. Conyea," said Ray. "Just gotta sit here patiently until the sun comes up."

"Call me George," said Conyea.

Ray nodded. Then each survivor settled in for a long night, lost in his own thoughts. Ray tried to make an honest assessment of their situation. They had no food or water. Once the sun came up, their thirst would increase, and dehydration would wear them down with each passing hour. The weather was calm, with just a light breeze, and for that Ray was thankful. If the seas had been rough, like the day before, none of them would have been able to hang on to the flimsy raft. They were lucky indeed to be in gentle swells rather than breaking waves. Because the waves were not large, none of the survivors were seasick. However, they had no flares to signal a plane or patrol boat that might appear on the horizon.

After days of traveling from South America on the *Heredia*, Ray had an appreciation for the vastness of the ocean. He felt that the little raft was like the proverbial needle in a haystack: it was going to be difficult to find. And a person in the water without a raft would be nearly impossible to locate. Ray said a silent prayer that Ina and Lucille were together on a raft and not alone in the endless void of the sea.

∼

Around five in the morning, Sonny was shivering slightly. He could hardly believe how slowly the night was passing. It seemed like it had been days ago that the *Heredia* was torpedoed. He knew he was supposed to tell his father if he was cold, but he thought it best not to say anything for a while. The grown-ups had stopped talking, but every now and then Sonny's dad would ask how he was doing.

"Sonny, it will be dawn soon, and we'll all get a chance to warm up in the sun."

"Yes, Dad, I, I . . . know."

Ray picked up the hesitation in the boy's voice, and he could tell Sonny was shaking.

"Mr. Conyea—I mean, George," said Ray, "I'm going to have Sonny come sit with me, so you may need to shift position slightly."

"Okay; it will be good to move. My back is as stiff as can be."

Ray slid down to the end of his side of the raft closest to Sonny's side, and then said, "Sonny, you can scoot over to me now."

The boy had no trouble sliding to his father. It was wonderful to feel his dad's muscular arm pull him in tight so that he was leaning into his dad's chest. Sonny could relax, and he began to examine the luminescence where the gentle swells swirled around the raft. On board the ship, his father had called the eerie light *phosphorescence*, and Sonny was fascinated by the glowing plankton that shimmered in the night.

Feeling secure in his father's embrace, the boy closed his eyes for the first time since the ship had been torpedoed. He must have dozed for a few minutes but was awakened by a commotion.

"I've got it," said Captain Colburn.

Sonny could see that the captain had something large in his hands, but the boy had no idea what it was.

"What's happening, Dad?"

"We saw a board floating on the water, and the captain was able to grab it. Might come in handy in the morning. Maybe use it as a paddle."

~

U-boat Commander Würdemann

The same night that he torpedoed the *Heredia*, Commander Würdemann saw a small freighter on an easterly course. This ship was lucky. The young commander estimated that he could not get in position before daylight, and he let the ship sail away. U-506 submerged. Würdemann was content with the prize of sinking the *Heredia* . . . for now. He still had more torpedoes.

The commander didn't have to wait long for his next target. The *Halo*, a 7,000-ton tanker loaded with oil, was zigzagging in a rapidly changing pattern, making it a much more difficult target than the *Heredia*. But Würdemann knew that this was a loaded tanker, a real prize, and although the ship came in and out of sight, he doggedly pursued it. When he finally was within 450 meters, he ordered two torpedoes fired.

"After twenty-one seconds," the commander wrote in his diary, "[the torpedoes] hit forward edge of the bridge and center. Tanker bursts into flames and in just a moment is a torch. A heavy internal explosion follows. Apparently the tanker is torn apart in the middle. Details cannot be distinguished in the bright fiery flare." Würdemann watched his prize burn for a few minutes, then "dived, ran off." But an hour later his curiosity got the better of him, and he surfaced in a different location, farther away and confirmed that the ship had indeed sunk and that "burning oil can still be seen some time on the water."

While most of the *Halo*'s sailors survived the initial explosion by jumping into the sea, help was slow in coming, as the ship did not get off an SOS. Over the next few days, men began dying of exposure. Of the 42 crew members, one was rescued after five days and two were picked up after seven days of clinging to a half-burned raft. The other 39 crew members perished.

Within hours of sinking the *Halo*, Würdemann spotted two freighters and used his last three torpedoes in a vain attempt to sink them. With the first freighter, Würdemann thought he had miscalculated the freighter's speed, but the second left him scratching his head. "Both [torpedoes] missed, unexplained with low range and good data. From sound, both torpedoes ran perfectly."

While the commander was miffed at this waste of torpedoes, the crew was likely thinking of home. They had been at sea for 45 days, and their time in the Gulf was especially difficult because of the intense heat. It felt as if they were in the mouth of a dragon. No one had bathed during the trip, and condensation formed inside the sub, adding a clammy feeling to the men's stinking bodies. All the fresh food had been consumed, and the men were living on rice and gruel.

The crew had survived depth charges dropped by enemy

aircraft and a near grounding off the mouth of the Mississippi, but it was the day-to-day challenges of being locked inside a steel tube that wore down even the most gung-ho sailor. Würdemann was a rare exception. He had used up all his torpedoes and set a course to return to Lorient, yet he still hoped to bag another ship by using his deck guns. As U-506 plowed eastward, the commander sent a short message to Lorient, encouraging his superiors to send more U-boats to the area. "Off Mississippi continuous heavy independent traffic. Certainly worthwhile for other boats. Constant air, however no sea patrol determined."

15

DAWN

INA (FIFTH HOUR IN THE OCEAN)

Morning's gray light crept across the sky. Ina could no longer see any sign of the *Heredia* or the U-boat that had sunk it, just debris in the water. After a few minutes, with sunlight now breaking through hazy clouds, she thought she could make out the shapes of people in the distance, sitting on a raft of flotsam.

Her hopes soared. Ina's vision, however, was badly blurred by the oil in her eyes, so she wasn't sure if the shapes really were survivors. Her left eye stung, and her eyelid was almost sealed shut. She said a silent prayer, wiped at her eyes with an oily hand, and then kicked her legs to get closer to the shapes.

When she was 20 feet away, she could hear the group talking, and she called out, "Sonny! Lucille! Ray!"

"We're sailors!" came the response. "We'll help you."

The sailors were sitting on a large piece of wood that likely had come from the *Heredia*. Holding on to her tiny board, Ina kicked toward the sailors and asked, "Have you seen my husband and children?"

"No, ma'am," the two sailors responded. One slipped into the water, keeping his naked body out of sight. They all looked around at the horizon, helping Ina scan the bobbing debris for her family. The heaps of broken wood and scattered pieces of the ship's equipment were thinning out with time and the pull of wind and currents. Nobody wanted to guess if she'd ever see her family again.

~

LUCILLE (FIFTH AND SIXTH HOURS IN THE OCEAN)

Lucille, drifting over a mile away from her mother, also saw the arrival of dawn. A cloudless sky slowly brightened to reveal a scene of destruction as far as Lucille could see. She shivered at the sight of pieces of wreckage, the dead body of a sailor floating facedown in the distance, and a dull gray sheen on the water where oil stained the surface.

As the makeshift raft rocked up and over small swells, its occupants scanned the horizon: no sign of ships, rescuers, or Lucille's family. The sailors in the water around Lucille's raft did their best to stay warm and alert, knowing that drifting off to sleep might kill them.

Lucille laughed and said, "Hey, Mr. Roy, quit tickling me."

"Tickling you?" asked the second mate.

"Yes, my feet."

"Maybe you could shift over here a bit and bring your feet up on the raft," Sorli suggested. "That will make it easier for me to tickle them."

Sorli had seen the large shape of a shark beneath them and knew that was what had brushed up against Lucille's feet. He would do his best to keep her from looking down and discovering what was there.

Lucille started to hum. The men encouraged her to sing, and she sang one of the church songs that her mother liked.

To pass the time, Sorli proceeded to teach Lucille the meanings of many of the signal flags and how they could be combined to convey a ship's circumstances.

The second mate knew how to make the best of a bad situation. He didn't want to talk in depth about his home and family because many of the memories were painful. Roy was the youngest of 12 children who had learned to work hard at an early age on his family's subsistence farm north of the Arctic Circle. Long, sunless winters forced him and his siblings to make up games to entertain themselves when they had free time. His father had been a harsh taskmaster, and leaving home at 16 had seemed like Roy's only option. Yet Roy Sorli was a gentle soul who sought quiet companionship, and he worshipped his fiancée, who he knew would worry when she didn't hear from him that day. Distracting Lucille was also distracting himself, keeping the sailor from worrying that his future plans might not come to pass.

~

SONNY AND RAY

(FIFTH AND SIXTH HOURS IN THE OCEAN)

A faint hint of dawn enabled red-haired Captain Colburn to better see his bleak surroundings. The gray canvas-covered raft seemed minuscule and so flimsy that he wondered how long it would take for the fabric to rip and the balsa wood to float free. He glanced at his shipwrecked mates. George Conyea appeared exhausted, and he had said very little during the night. The boy, Sonny, hadn't cried once, but he looked so small and skinny that the captain knew he must be extremely cold. His father, Ray, had calmed down since he'd thought he heard his wife shouting, and he was now holding the boy close to his chest.

It crossed the captain's mind that the four of them might be the only survivors of the ship. If that were true, his own survival would become a lifelong burden and source of shame rather than a blessing. He imagined what the newspapers would say and what other mariners would think. It would look bad when they learned that of the entire crew of *Heredia,* he, the captain, was the only one who lived. That would mean 49 of his crew had perished, six of the Navy Armed Guard, and three out of the six passengers—all on his vessel, on his watch, during his leadership. He knew that the notion that the captain should go down with the ship was still strong. *But*, he thought, *at least these three civilians on the raft with me can testify that we were the very last ones off the ship.* It didn't ease his anguish, but it was something.

Colburn had also been thinking about sharks on and off all night, doing his best to put the predators out of his mind. But when Ray Downs shifted positions slightly, the captain's eyes widened. In the gloom he saw a dark smudge on Ray Downs's knee.

"Is that blood or oil on your leg?" asked the captain.

"Blood," said Ray. "I cut myself trying to break through the window."

"Let me help you cover the wound. I can tear off a piece of my shirt."

"I can get it," answered Ray. "We've got the raft pretty well balanced, and the less moving around, the better."

Ray wore only a sleeveless T-shirt and his boxer shorts. He ripped a small patch of cloth from his T-shirt to tie around the cut.

Sonny watched his father's hands work. The gash looked deep, and even after Roy had been in the ocean more than three hours, the wound was still trickling blood.

"How bad does it hurt, Dad?"

"Can barely feel it. Salt water stings a bit. This bulky life jacket bothers me as much as the cut, the way it's rubbing against my skin. I'll bet your life jacket is doing the same."

Early in 1942, the U.S. coasts were lightly defended, allowing German U-boats to prey on ship traffic even during daytime. Tankers like this one were targets because the Germans sought to block fuel needed for the war effort.

German submarines, called U-boats, were stealthy war machines that could cross an ocean and spend weeks torpedoing ships before returning to their bases.
Uboatarchive.net

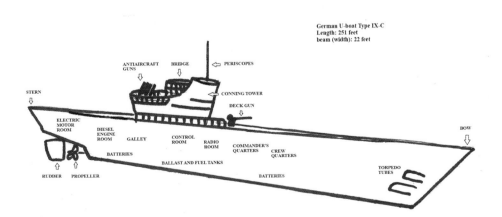

German U-boat Type IX-C
Length: 251 feet
beam (width): 22 feet

ANTIAIRCRAFT GUNS
BRIDGE
PERISCOPES
STERN
CONNING TOWER
DECK GUN
ELECTRIC MOTOR ROOM
DIESEL ENGINE ROOM
GALLEY
CONTROL ROOM
RADIO ROOM
COMMANDER'S QUARTERS
CREW QUARTERS
BOW
BATTERIES
BALLAST AND FUEL TANKS
BATTERIES
TORPEDO TUBES
RUDDER
PROPELLER

The *Heredia* was owned by the United Fruit Company, and its holds were filled with coffee and bananas on its final voyage from South America to New Orleans, Louisiana, in 1942. The Downs family and two other men were the only civilians aboard when the German U-boat U-506 fired torpedoes into its hull and sank the ship in the Gulf of Mexico, about 40 miles offshore.

It took months for the United States and its allies to develop defenses to stop German U-boats, including depth charges that were dropped from airplanes like the long-range B24 Liberator.

Getting ready for the family's adventurous move to South America in 1941 included having pictures taken for passports. In this portrait, Ina Downs is flanked by her sons, Raymond Jr. (Sonny) on the left and Terry on the right. Next to Terry is Betty Lucille.
Courtesy of the Downs family.

Ina Downs left many letters to family members and a recording about her experiences in South America and aboard the ship *Heredia* when it was torpedoed. She was traveling with her husband and two children when the ship sank in the Gulf of Mexico.

Courtesy of the Downs family.

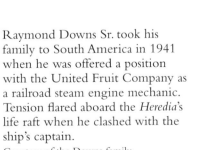

Raymond Downs Sr. took his family to South America in 1941 when he was offered a position with the United Fruit Company as a railroad steam engine mechanic. Tension flared aboard the *Heredia*'s life raft when he clashed with the ship's captain.

Courtesy of the Downs family.

Admiral Karl Dönitz was the mastermind behind the aggressive German U-boat offensive off the East Coast of the United States in 1942.

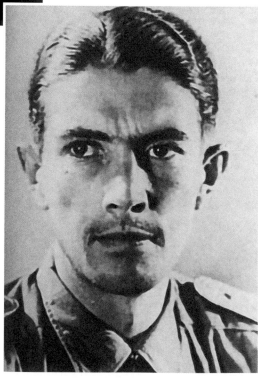

Erich Würdemann was the commander of the German submarine U-506, which waged successful attacks against American shipping vessels along the East Coast and in the Gulf of Mexico, including the torpedoing of the *Heredia* at 2:00 A.M. on May 19, 1942.

Harro Schacht was the gregarious commander of U-507, a German submarine that sank many ships in the Gulf of Mexico during 1942, and then went on to do the same in Brazilian waters, killing 500 people in a short period.
Uboatarchive.net

The Downs family was reunited in the Morgan City hospital after about 20 hours clinging to rafts and shipwreck debris in the Gulf of Mexico.
Courtesy of the Downs family.

Sonny was eight years old and Lucille was 11 when the ship they were on was torpedoed by a German submarine in the Gulf of Mexico. They were lucky to survive with just scrapes.
Courtesy of the Downs family.

The *Heredia*'s second mate, Roy Sorli, received the Merchant Marine Meritorious Service Medal for saving Lucille's life after the ship was torpedoed and sunk in the Gulf of Mexico.
Courtesy of the Sorli family.

"I don't mind. I'm sure glad I had it on when we were climbing up the stairway from our cabin. I felt like I was being dragged to the bottom of the sea."

"Me, too," said Ray. "I tried to hold on to you, but the water just yanked you away."

"Did you try and grab my leg?"

"Don't remember. Everything happened so fast."

"Something grabbed my leg and scared me, so I kicked at it. Hope it wasn't you. Hope it wasn't Mom or Lucille."

Ray winced. The thought of Ina and Lucille being pulled to the depths was more than he could handle. He had never been religious like his wife, but now he said a silent prayer. He thought it was a miracle that he had escaped the sinking ship, and maybe God did have a hand in his survival so he could be here with his son. Mixed with these thoughts of God was a brooding anger that bubbled to his consciousness periodically. His most intense fury was directed at the Germans on the submarine. They had crossed an entire ocean and most of the Gulf to hunt down and torpedo a ship that wasn't even part of the military. *They will pay for this*, he thought. *Nobody hurts my family and gets away with it.*

While the adrenaline prompted by thoughts of revenge coursed through Ray's veins, he also felt rage toward another group. That anger was directed at those in Corpus Christi who wouldn't let his family leave the *Heredia* when it anchored outside the bay. He wondered if the captain had really made a strong effort to persuade those authorities to let the family disembark.

Now, sitting on this floating sandbox just four feet from the captain, Ray struggled to keep from giving voice to his thoughts.

He looked down at the top of his son's head and held him tighter. As much for himself as for Sonny, Ray corralled his emotions and said, "Your mom and Lucille are probably floating with a bunch of the ship's sailors. They might even have been rescued by now."

With the innocence of an eight-year-old, Sonny believed his father. *Lucille is probably having breakfast onboard a rescue boat and she's worried about me. And Mom's likely right by her side, just the way Dad is with me.*

But a few minutes later, Sonny remembered that his dad had thought he heard his mother shouting when they were still near the sinking ship. *Maybe they are not with sailors or rescued.* Sonny was about to say something, to remind his father about his mother shouting for help, but he decided it was best to let it go. *Don't upset him.*

Sonny wanted his father to be proud of what he said and did while on the raft.

Now that the boy could grasp the vast size of the ocean and their own insignificance in it, he felt fear and dread. It was a helpless feeling, similar to what he'd felt when he had been washed from his father's grip as the ship lurched. Sonny didn't want his father to know that he felt like crying.

Captain Colburn admired the way the boy and his father interacted. He wasn't so sure about how things would go if a major decision needed to be made on the raft. He was still smarting from the exchange with Ray when they were launching the raft, the way Ray had poked him in the chest and shouted that he'd have to learn to swim real fast. Now adrift on the raft, where minutes felt like hours, he wondered if they'd have another disagreement. His ship might be at the bottom of the ocean, but he was still the captain.

16

DESPERATION

(MORNING INTO AFTERNOON)

When dawn broke at the busy shipping port of New Orleans and the *Heredia* did not appear at its expected time, there was no sense of alarm. The port officials knew that a vessel could be late for a variety of reasons, and under the restrictions of radio silence, the captain had no way to update them on his progress. While there had been U-boat attacks on ships in the Gulf almost daily, the *Heredia* had not sent out a mayday and no other vessels nearby had broken the radio silence with a report of either a ship in distress or an explosion.

~

Sonny and Ray (Seventh, Eighth, and Ninth Hours in the Ocean)

The gray life raft and the four survivors rose and fell with the endless swells. Each time it reached the crest, the three adults scanned the ocean in every direction, hoping against all odds that they might spot a ship. The captain had managed to retain his binoculars through the tumultuous night, but they were of limited use, as the horizon remained empty of ships. As the sun's rays gained strength, Sonny was able to leave his father's arms and perch on the edge of the raft with his legs dangling underwater in the raft's middle.

"The sun feels good," said Ray. "I don't care what people say about the warmth of the Gulf Stream: This water is cold."

George Conyea agreed. "If and when I warm up, I'm going to slip into the water just so I can stretch my back. Can only sit for so long."

Sonny was also stiff and cold, but he did not like the thought of being back in the water.

Captain Colburn's voice brought him out of his gloomy thoughts.

"Way off to the east, I think I see a plane. It's hard to see with the sun, but I think it's coming this way."

Everyone immediately looked east, squinting into the sun's glare. "Yes! Yes!" shouted Ray. "I can see it. Quick," he barked, looking at the captain, "give me your coat! Let's get it on the board!"

The captain's white jacket was draped over the board, and Ray held the makeshift flag as high as he could and then waved it back and forth.

Sonny thought for sure that the pilot, even though far off in that plane, would easily see it.

The plane was more than a mile away. Sonny held his hand over his eyes to block the sun. He was literally holding his breath. He stared until he could no longer see the speck in the blue sky.

Ray slowly lowered the board.

George Conyea broke the silence. "Maybe there'll be others. That one was just too far away."

Ray and the captain nodded, but neither spoke.

Conyea continued, "Sure wish we had a flare."

Sonny figured that now that it was daylight, another plane would come by in a few minutes. The boy didn't truly realize the danger he was in. He thought that because his father was with him he would be safe. Yes, he was cold, thirsty, and hungry, but it was nothing that he couldn't handle for a few more minutes. His father didn't show a trace of fear, so Sonny assumed he had the situation under control and it would all work out.

Later in the morning, the group spied a ship in the distance, and the captain took his coat off, placed it on the board, and kept it ready to wave when the ship got closer.

Sonny got a glimpse of the ship whenever the raft crested a swell, but when the swell passed and the raft descended into the wave's trough it was blocked from view by the water. Each time the raft rose to the top of the swell, he spotted the ship but couldn't tell if it was steaming toward them: it was just a little bump on the horizon. Eventually he tired of looking at it.

A few minutes later, the captain took his jacket off the plank and draped it over his head to protect his fair, freckled face and neck from the sun's damaging brilliance. No one needed to say the ship was moving in the wrong direction, and the group remained silent.

The ocean, taking on a gray-green hue under the climbing sun, stretched out as empty as a desert. Their only salvation would be from either a ship or a plane. Ray cursed the designers of the life raft. Why had they not dyed the gray canvas a brighter color so it could more easily be spotted? He imagined himself on a passing ship far off in the distance and knew it would be virtually impossible to see this tiny raft. Half the time it would be hidden from view by the swells. He reckoned a ship would need to be within a quarter mile for any crew member to have a shot at spotting the captain's white coat on the board. And even if someone did see it, they might think it was flotsam drifting up and over the swells.

~

INA (SIXTH THROUGH TENTH HOURS IN THE OCEAN)

Ina was glad she had found the sailors, because they helped take her mind off her family. They shared stories: One sailor had been on watch, the other in the shower when the torpedo hit. Both had been blown free of the ship. They were lucky to have found the big board. Ina and one sailor sat on top of this board with their feet in the water. Sometimes they lay down on it and held on tight so the small waves would not knock them off. The sailor who was naked continued to stay in the water, only gripping this board with his fingers. Ina noticed his hands turning white as he struggled to continue holding on to this board. He was also shivering, but he was unwilling to bare his body in front of a woman.

"Sailor, get back on this board," Ina said. "This is no time for modesty."

"No, ma'am, I'm fine. I'm just resting my back," he responded.

Ina worried that the young man would die from hypothermia. "If you don't get on this board," said Ina, "I'm going to go off on my own."

The sailor stayed in the water.

Incredibly, Ina decided to leave the board so the naked sailor would climb on it.

"Well, I suppose I'll keep looking for my children. God bless." Then she slid off the large board and slowly swam away, clutching a small piece of wood.

At least without me there, Ina thought, *the sailor will get back on the planks and have a chance to live.*

The chill of the night had been replaced by the blazing rays of the sun, but Ina decided not to shed her heavy coat, wondering if she could survive another night in water that sucked away her body's warmth. Being adrift in the ocean was terrifying, but even worse were the thoughts about her family and the very real possibility that they had gone down with the ship. *Don't think that way*, she scolded herself; *if I escaped, somehow they did, too.* She'd go mad with grief if she thought the worst had happened. She knew to put such negative thoughts out of her mind and focus on saving herself so she could search for her family.

Soon Ina found another pair of survivors: a Filipino sailor who clung to a board, half-conscious, and a ship's officer who'd stayed with him all night, treading water and holding the sailor's head up to keep him alive. "Have you seen my family?" she inquired.

"No, ma'am, I'm sorry," said the officer. "And, please, beware of the debris. Some of these boards are sharp. If you bump into them and they cut you, the sharks will come and pick your bones."

She wondered about the men's chances for survival as she paddled on in search of her family. Far in the distance Ina thought she could make out the silhouette of a ship, and she began paddling toward it. After ten minutes, she was out of breath and her arms hung like dead weights over the front of the narrow board she clutched to her chest. The life vest and the heavy coat made paddling especially difficult. She contemplated removing her coat and letting it sink to the depths, but her intuition told her to keep it, no matter how bulky and cumbersome. She did, however, stop paddling, realizing that she would never make it to the object on the horizon and was needlessly tiring herself.

How much longer will it be until help arrives? she wondered. The officer's warning about sharks was causing havoc with her imagination, and she shuddered at the thought. Then she saw some cork in the water and panicked, thinking her life preserver had ruptured and wouldn't keep her afloat much longer. Despair clung to the edges of every thought, so Ina tried not to think at all. But it was impossible; her mind went straight back to her family, trying to calculate their odds of survival and the chance for rescue. Surely the authorities knew by now that the ship not only was overdue but also had been sunk. Yet if that was the case, why weren't there planes overhead or patrol boats in the area? Just thinking about the people "in charge" on land made her furious. Sonny, Lucille, Raymond, and she could have all gotten off at Corpus Christi if the officials had had an ounce of common sense.

~

LUCILLE (ELEVENTH THROUGH FIFTEENTH HOURS IN THE OCEAN)

Lucille was growing drowsy. It was now afternoon, and the young girl felt as if she had been in the ocean for days rather than just 12 hours.

The sailors took turns holding on to Lucille's little raft, which provided more support than the waterlogged life vests that some of them had had time to grab before the ship went down. She helped them by pointing out jellyfish drifting nearby so they could defend their exposed skin by pushing the creatures away with pieces of wood. She glimpsed a shark below the raft now and then but never realized that was what had been tickling her feet in the darkness. Sorli had seen the predator and a couple of others much earlier, so when Lucille nervously pointed out the shark, he was ready with soothing words. "It's harmless; just a little curious about what we're doing out here."

That was good enough for Lucille. If Mr. Roy wasn't concerned, she wouldn't be, either.

"Suppose the captain made it out?" Robello asked no one in particular.

"Don't know. I was on the bridge with him when we were hit," said Sorli. "He had about the same chance as I did."

"The codes? Papers?"

"There was no time to take them from the cabinet and put them in the bag," Sorli said of the procedure of ensuring that the secret naval codes would be destroyed if a ship were abandoned.

"It only took me thirty seconds to put my shoes on, but the deck was awash the minute I stepped outside. Do you suppose we had time to transmit?" asked Burke. Then he answered his own question. "No, never mind. I know the answer. The first torpedo hit amidships. There was no time; the radioman must have been killed instantly. Poor guy."

Silence again descended on the group. They wondered if surviving the attack would turn out to be a blessing or a curse. Like many shipwreck survivors, they might struggle to stay alive only to suffer longer at the merciless whim of the elements. Without food a person could live for days, but without fresh water, that time would be much shorter.

The effects of hypothermia, even in the Gulf's mild temperatures, were already being felt, as it takes only a few hours for hands, feet, and other extremities to experience numbness and lack of mobility, the first sign usually being slurred speech. It was one thing for a grown man to accept the dangers as part of his job, but watching a helpless child like Lucille suffer galvanized the group. They would do anything to ease her discomfort.

As the sun marched toward the western horizon, each of the sailors was summoning his energy for another cold night in the water, trying to assess the odds of lasting without water and with sharks circling beneath.

17

RUNNING OUT OF TIME

(LATE MORNING INTO AFTERNOON)

SONNY AND RAY (TENTH THROUGH
FOURTEENTH HOURS IN THE OCEAN)

Sonny asked if he could move off his father's lap and back to his original side of the raft. He needed to stretch and didn't feel quite so cold anymore.

A couple of hours passed in silence. Eventually Captain Colburn muttered, "We'd better be rescued before dark, because we're drifting into the shipping lanes, where there's a good chance we'll be run down."

Ray shot a piercing glance at Colburn, jerking his head toward his son as a warning. He didn't want the boy to hear any of this talk about being run over by a ship.

The sun was blazing hot on Sonny's bare skin, its rays amplified by bouncing off the water. He no longer felt quite as cold, but his little body had used a considerable amount of energy just to keep warm through the endless night. Simply shivering had consumed much of his limited supply of reserve strength. He felt tired and weak, similar to the way he'd felt while sick with the flu. Sonny didn't say anything, because he was determined to be as tough as his dad. Instead he simply asked if he could move back to sitting next to his father so he could lean against him.

"Yes, and lay your head against my side and maybe you can doze."

Sonny craved water, just a sip, and earlier had asked his father about taking in a mouthful from the ocean. Ray told him not to, that it would make him sick and that he'd have all the water he wanted when a rescue boat came. But Ray still kept a wary eye on his son, afraid the boy might take a small sip of seawater when he wasn't looking. It was an overwhelming, constant temptation for all four of the survivors, but drinking seawater would have had the opposite effect of what was needed.

The high sodium content of seawater would have dehydrated the castaways even quicker than having no water at all. The sodium in seawater needs to be expelled from the body. That means precious fluids from the muscles, other tissues, and organs are drawn off to produce urine. This natural process also takes place in brain tissue, and the resulting loss of hydration often causes delirium and hallucinations within an hour or two of consuming it. This altered mental state has caused more than one shipwrecked person to do the unthinkable—climb out of the life raft and start swimming toward an object they imagined was there.

In midafternoon, Sonny felt something brush up against his leg, and he looked down to find a green banana floating next to him. He grabbed the banana. "Look what I found," he exclaimed to his father.

"Good job. Better hang on to that in case we need it."

Sonny smiled. He was contributing.

The motion of the waves and the lack of conversation lulled the boy to sleep. The slumber didn't last long, because even in the sun he was chilled and his muscles cramped. When he awoke a half hour later, he realized he had dropped the banana, and felt devastated.

"Dad, I dropped the banana."

"Don't worry. You'll find it—or another one."

Sonny didn't think so. He could see absolutely nothing on the ocean's surface and knew that the only reason he'd found the banana in the first place was because it had bumped into his leg. Under the circumstances, it was more than a piece of fruit; Sonny viewed it as evidence that he was doing his part to keep everyone alive, so losing it was a terrible mistake. He fought to restrain his emotions.

Ray tried to cheer him up. "A while back when we were on the top of a swell, I thought I saw a couple of little specks on the horizon."

The captain joined in. "I'll bet they were shrimp boats, and one of them is bound to head our way."

Sonny wasn't so sure. Despite the sun burning his skin, he was cold again, and he felt weaker than ever.

~

By late afternoon, all three adults on the raft were concerned that they wouldn't be found before sundown. The specks on the horizon were gone, and no more planes came out of the cloudless sky. The landscape of ocean and sky was so bleak and empty that they felt like the only living things on the planet.

Their thirst had reached an unbearable level, and talking was now at a minimum. Parched mouths and throats made speaking difficult, and each survivor had turned inward. Ray knew he could get through a second night, but he wasn't so sure about Sonny. He worried that as the night wore on, the combination of dehydration and hypothermia would take its toll on the boy, and he might not be conscious by morning. Rescue, if it were coming at all, had to come soon.

The men took turns as lookout so the other two could close their eyes against the sun's burning glare. Sonny, too, kept his eyes closed but could not sleep. His skin felt like it was on fire, and his father did his best to use his own body to shield his son.

"Captain," said Ray, "my son needs your coat. His skin is burning."

Captain Colburn looked at the boy's skin, and it did not look red. Then he glanced at the boy's dark hair. "But I'm so fair-skinned, I really need it," Colburn replied.

There was an awkward silence. Sonny had heard the exchange and felt his father's body tense, and the boy sat up.

His father spoke in a tone he had not heard before: slow, measured, and very soft.

"Give him the coat," said Ray, "or I will throw you off this raft."

The captain looked like he'd been punched in the stomach. He started to say something, then stopped, took the jacket off, and tossed it to Ray.

A tense silence descended on the life raft. George Conyea averted his eyes from both Ray and the captain and simply stared at the horizon. He hadn't said a word since the morning. He wanted no part of the tension between the captain and Ray. Conyea was dealing with his own pain. His bald head had been burned by the morning sun, so he had taken off his shirt and covered his head with it. But now his bare back was as red as a tomato.

Ray felt like he was going to jump out of his skin. His mind kept circling back to Ina and Lucille, and the helplessness he felt ate away at him like acid. He had never sat in one place for as long as he'd done on the raft, and he needed to be doing something, doing anything to keep busy and take his mind off his wife and daughter. Minutes dragged by like hours. He felt that if the captain said one more word about anything at all, he'd erupt like a volcano.

Around four in the afternoon, Ray's back was aching so badly that he needed to straighten it. He told the others he was going to slip into the water the way George Conyea had earlier, and asked the group to steady themselves and do their best to keep the raft balanced. Ray inched forward and lowered himself into the middle of the raft. Then he turned so that only his arms were draped across the canvas and balsa wood on his side of the square. The cool water and a straightened back felt wonderful, and he floated in that position for several minutes before climbing back into the sitting position.

Ray asked Sonny if he wanted to do the same thing, but the boy said no. Sitting with the captain's jacket on had helped with the sun, and he was lost in his own exhausted stupor. Then he felt something against his leg. He glanced down and could not believe what he saw: a banana, perhaps the same one he had lost earlier, was bobbing in the water.

"Dad, look!" he shouted, reaching out and snatching the green banana.

"I knew you'd find it. I think that banana is really going to help us. Why don't you unpeel it and take a big bite and then pass it around for all of us to share?"

Sonny did as he was told. It was a struggle to swallow his piece of the banana with his mouth and throat so dry. Twenty seconds later, he felt nauseous and vomited the banana bite back into the sea.

"Well, that didn't work so well," Ray said. "The banana wasn't ripe, anyway."

Sonny only nodded. He was slumped forward with his head hanging so low that it almost reached his knees.

A few minutes later, Sonny said, "Dad, can we go in now?" He said it as if they were on a fishing trip and it was up to his father when to call it quits.

Rather than try to explain the situation, his father answered, "Soon, son, soon."

Sonny looked up at his father and just nodded.

It wasn't long after this exchange that Ray noticed Conyea staring at something directly behind where Ray was sitting. Ray turned his head and saw not one but four gray shark fins lazily cutting through the sea just five feet from the raft. When he looked over at Conyea and the captain, he saw another couple of fins. By now all four of the survivors could see the sharks. No one said a word.

One shark turned toward the raft and then glided directly under it. The group could see the outline of its body as it passed directly beneath them. It looked to be about five to six feet long.

Sonny quickly pulled his feet out of the water.

"Take it easy, Sonny. Don't thrash around," said his dad. "They'll move on."

But they didn't move on.

The four survivors now counted seven different sharks making slow half loops around the raft before passing directly underneath it. This was by far the most terrifying experience of the ordeal for both Sonny and the three adults. The raft was too small for the men to get their legs on top of the balsa wood. Ray was right: their best defense was not to make a commotion.

The men did not know what kind of sharks they were, only

that they appeared to be as big as the men on the raft. The Gulf of Mexico has over 40 different species of shark, but the ones the group should have been most worried about were bull sharks, hammerhead sharks, tiger sharks, oceanic whitetip sharks, dusky sharks, and of course great white sharks. Because of the shape of these sharks, the hammerhead could be ruled out, as could the great white, bull shark, and tiger shark because they are usually solitary hunters. It's also probable that the sharks were not the oceanic whitetip, because the dorsal fin the survivors saw was a solid gray.

The sharks circling the raft might have been dusky sharks, which are known to hunt in packs, often corralling their prey and then taking turns darting in to take a bite. And their bite is among the strongest of any shark on the planet. While not as aggressive as the bull shark, tiger shark, or great white shark, dusky sharks have attacked and killed humans and are considered among the most dangerous to humans.

The life raft probably acted like a magnet for sharks, attracting their interest simply because it was a floating object. Also, the sharks, with their keen sense of smell, could have been drawn by the scent of blood from Ray's wound. And any movement the group made, such as switching position, caused vibrations in the water, making the sharks curious. It's also possible that smaller fish were staying under the shade of the raft; the sharks had come to investigate this potential prey and then became inquisitive about the humans.

Several castaways have reported that circling sharks may slowly move closer and then bump and nudge a raft, perhaps to see if the raft is a living thing. Over time, the sharks become more aggressive. Instead of a gentle bump, they slam into the raft. Some survivors say that once sharks realize there is something living on the raft, they try to flip the vessel to get at its occupants.

Sonny didn't know any of this. All he knew was that the great beasts were just a few feet away. And they were getting closer as the minutes crawled on.

18

SHARKS, DOLPHINS, AND BIRDS FAR AWAY

(AFTERNOON)

SONNY AND RAY (FIFTEENTH AND SIXTEENTH HOURS IN THE OCEAN)

The sharks circled the *Heredia* survivors silently in a mesmerizing, menacing swirl of sleek bodies and fins, moving closer with every loop. They made lazy half loops just a couple of feet off the side of the raft before submerging and swimming directly under it. One shark, when passing under the raft, rolled onto its back, and an anxious Sonny could see its half-opened mouth. The boy almost let out a scream, but his dad, who had seen the same thing, reached over and put his hand on Sonny's shoulder.

"Don't worry, they are just checking us out. We are something new to them."

Ray had no idea if that statement was true, but he didn't want his son to panic. He hoped his words calmed the captain and George Conyea, too, because they were as wide-eyed as Sonny, watching every move their new visitors made.

Ray felt despair like he had never known. Sundown was just three and a half hours away. Thinking of the sharks gliding beneath them at night was too terrible to imagine. He felt absolutely helpless.

Minutes crawled by and the four survivors kept still, eyes glued on the fins lazily cutting through the water on all sides of the raft. The behavior of the sharks stayed the same; they came within a foot or two of the castaways but made no direct contact with either the raft or the group's legs or feet.

"How long will they stay?" asked Sonny, looking at his father.

"Don't know, Sonny; but like I said, they are just curious." Ray paused and continued his calming words: "If we don't bother them, they won't bother us."

George Conyea spoke up for the first time in quite a while. "Do you know what kind they are?"

"Probably harmless sand sharks," Ray responded. In reality he still did not know. Ray had spent little time on the ocean, and this was an entirely new experience. If the captain knew more than Ray, he didn't say so.

An hour went by and the group tried to ignore the sharks, but with little success. There was nothing else to look at, nothing else to take their mind off the seven fins circling them.

About two hours after the first sharks arrived, more fins

appeared in the water not far from the raft. Sonny was terrified, thinking, *More sharks* . . .

Captain Colburn spoke up. "Hey, those are dolphins."

Like the U-boat that had caused their ordeal, the sharks submerged and were not seen again.

Sonny experienced great relief and joy with the dolphins' arrival and the sharks' departure. He felt as if he had been holding his breath for the past two hours, afraid to move a muscle. There was no doubt in his mind that the dolphins had driven the sharks off to help him.

It's doubtful that the dolphins were intentionally trying to save the lives of the humans, but rather, like the sharks, they were curious about the raft. Luckily, their presence caused the sharks to move off. Little is known about the dynamics between sharks and dolphins. Some researchers think the sound dolphins make can drive away sharks, while others think the dolphins' ability to work as a team can thwart sharks. Over the years there have been many accounts of castaways saying they were being shadowed by a shark only to have dolphins "chase the shark away." But dolphins are not always the dominant species; sharks will attack and eat a dolphin, given the chance.

~

The dolphins not only relieved Sonny's concern over the sharks but also gave him something new to watch. Unlike the sharks, the dolphins swam quickly around the raft. Their entire backs almost came out of the water, and then they briefly submerged and repeated the process. Up and down came their fins. But after just three or four minutes, they moved on and were gone from sight.

The group didn't speak. Without the fear of sharks, their minds went back to the predicament of time for a rescue running out. It would be dark within the hour. Their thirst was unbearable, and all felt extremely weak. Sonny was in the worst shape because of his small body. Now that the sun was low in the sky, he was shivering again. His father noticed and moved him closer, wrapping his big arms around the boy to stop his shaking.

Sonny looked up at his father. "Shouldn't a boat be here by now?" he asked.

Ray needed to keep his son's mind occupied. Instead of discussing the lack of a rescue boat, he said, "Let's play a game. See those seagulls way up there? You choose one and I'll choose one, and we'll count how long they go without flapping their wings. Whoever's bird flies the longest without using its wings wins."

"Okay, I'm picking the one over there," Sonny said as he lethargically pointed at a shape off to the west.

"And I've got the one straight up," answered Ray.

With their heads tilted back, father and son watched the birds they had chosen. It was easy to look up because the sun was almost touching the ocean.

"Mine just flapped," said Ray. "You win."

Sonny gave a half-hearted nod.

~

INA (ELEVENTH TO SIXTEENTH HOURS
IN THE OCEAN)

Ina didn't have anyone to help take her mind off her suffering. She was lost in thought about the hopelessness of her predicament when something tugged on her tattered nightgown, which swayed in the water, trailing behind her. She looked below and saw several pilot fish nibbling her nightgown and swimming between her legs. Then, with her blurred vision, she saw much larger shapes pass beneath her. Sharks! She could see about six of the creatures, each four to five feet long, lazily plying the waters under and around her. Panic and anger at her predicament welled up once again. And now she was on her own, without sailors to help her.

"Damn you to hell!" she shrieked, swinging a piece of wood at the fish, slapping the water. She kicked her legs and screamed, frenzied by the helpless feeling of losing her family and fearing a terrible death.

The sharks and pilot fish moved off a bit but stayed within sight. *They're like vultures*, she thought, *just waiting for me to weaken further.*

Ina tugged the remains of her nightgown in tight and then pulled down on her heavy coat. Next she brought her legs up so that her knees were near her chest. She didn't want her legs dangling below and thought the coat offered a measure of protection. The sharks had pushed her to the breaking point. *Dear Lord*, she prayed, *I don't want to wait here for the sharks to get me . . . Better to just have it over with quick.*

When she looked back down, she could see only a couple of sharks and pilot fish.

Ina thought maybe it was God who had prompted her to keep the heavy coat when logic told her to discard it. Now she renewed her determination to live as long as the Lord wanted her to.

Later, the last of the sharks and pilot fish moved off. But the ordeal had left her shaken and feeling utterly depleted of all strength. The emptiness of the ocean settled back around her, sealing out noise and feeling. By midafternoon, with the sun's glare adding to the pain from her oil- and salt-encrusted eyes, she began to doubt that anyone was even searching for her. Ina worried that she had drifted far from the accident scene and would never be found. She craved water; her mouth was parched and her lips cracked. Oil-soaked clothing clung to her upper body while her bare legs dangled in the water below.

Ina looked at the empty blue sky and remembered the beautiful sunsets she'd seen while on the ship and how they had inspired her. Now the same sky seemed so blank and unforgiving. Her faith that God was with her was wavering. She tried to summon the energy to pray, to be thankful she was still alive, but she was too spent.

Another, larger board drifted nearby, perhaps part of a banana crate, and it was a welcome find. Ina pushed herself on top of the floating planks, getting most of her body out of the water for the first time in a dozen hours. She struggled with negative thoughts about her family's fate and about sharks in the water below.

SOMETHING IN THE SKY

(LATE AFTERNOON TO DUSK)

SONNY AND RAY

(SEVENTEENTH HOUR IN THE OCEAN)

Ray wasn't sure the "seagull game" was helping Sonny, but he figured it couldn't hurt.

"Well, let's play another round," said Ray.

Again they chose birds. Sonny chose one high in the sky and way off on the eastern horizon. This time the captain and George Conyea also looked up to see which birds the father and son chose. Anything to take their minds off their bodies' demands for water.

Ray's bird soon flapped its wings. "You win again," he said.

Sonny kept his eyes on his own bird. "Wow, Dad, mine is still going along without flapping."

Ray looked closer at the bird in the distance.

"Captain, let me use your binoculars," Ray said.

The captain removed the strap from around his neck and handed the binoculars to Ray, who hurriedly put them to his eyes. He adjusted the focus and stared intently at the bird far in the distance.

"That's no seagull—it's a plane!" he shouted.

"Yes, yes!" shouted the captain.

The survivors still could not hear its engines or tell what kind of plane it was, but there was no doubt it was a plane and that it was heading toward the raft.

"Quick, Sonny, take off the captain's coat! I've got to get it on the board."

Within seconds, Ray was waving the board with the white coat on it, and the others were waving their arms.

Ray couldn't tell if the pilot had spotted the white coat, and the tension was unbearable. *Please, please*, he said to himself. His son's life was at stake. The boy could not make it through another cold night. Ray waved the white coat wildly.

As the plane drew closer, its metal skin briefly glittered when the sun's rays hit it. Now they could hear the dull drone of the engine, and Sonny shouted, "Help!"

"Keep waving the flag!" shouted the captain, his excitement growing. "It's got to see us. It's our last chance! I think it's coming our way."

Ray could make out the outline of the plane and realized, because of its unique construction, that it was a U.S. Navy PBY. The letters *PB* stood for *Patrol Bomber*, and the *Y* was the designated code given to its manufacturer. It was also known as a flying boat because it could land on the water. The single wing was elevated above the main body of the aircraft rather than below the cockpit windows. This allowed unobstructed visibility for its aviators to scan the ocean during patrols for U-boats or search-and-rescue missions. Two engines with propellers were mounted on the wing, one on each side of the aircraft.

The plane came ever closer, but it did not descend. Ray thought maybe it was going too fast to see them.

Sonny's heart soared. He was certain the plane was coming for them. And he was right. In one swift motion, the PBY started descending and adjusting its course slightly so it was just 15 feet off the ocean. It headed right toward the raft, then banked hard; Sonny could actually see the pilot, who was giving a thumbs-up. The boy let out a croak of joy along with the cheers of his father, the captain, and George Conyea.

The four raft passengers watched with awe as the plane circled back toward them. Its 104-foot wingspan and 63-foot length made it appear enormous so close to the water. As the plane was barreling over their location, they saw the pilot drop a package out the window, landing just 10 feet from the raft. Using the board and their hands, all four survivors paddled furiously toward what they hoped was their salvation floating in the water.

The captain grabbed the package and ripped it open. Inside

were two flares, a large container of water, and a note. The captain read the note out loud: "We will send shrimp boats to come and get you. If anyone is seriously hurt, wave me in and I'll pick them up."

Ray thought for a minute. He knew the plane was going to search for other survivors in the few minutes of daylight left, and he didn't want to slow it down. Someone, maybe Lucille or Ina, might be hurt, and the plane could rescue them. He thought Sonny could make it the half hour or hour that he expected it would take the shrimp boat to arrive.

The plane made a broad circle above the raft and then moved off.

"We made it, son," said Ray. "We'll be on a boat in no time."

Then the captain passed the water container to Ray, saying, "Let's all take a small drink. We may want to let our bodies adjust to the water before we take a second drink."

When Sonny took his gulp of water, he thought he had never tasted anything so good, so sweet. It was as if the water had magical powers, because he felt better immediately. He couldn't wait for the container to come around for his second drink of the life-giving fluid. But the captain said again that they shouldn't drink too much all at once, and the other adults agreed.

A few minutes later the plane reappeared, then moved off. The survivors had no way of knowing that the pilot had dropped a note to shrimp boats a few miles off that said: "Watch my direction. Follow me. Pick up survivors in water."

A half hour went by and the survivors bobbed on their little raft in the darkening shadows. They all had another drink of water, and the captain said that he thought a shrimp boat could reach them within the next half hour.

Sonny shivered in his father's arms. The hydrating water had eased his thirst but did nothing for his growing hypothermia.

"That plane can land on water, right, Dad?"

"Yes."

"Then why didn't they just do that and pick us up?"

"They needed more time in the air to find others. But a boat will be here soon."

"What if the boat can't find us?"

"They will. And remember, we've got flares to use if we see a boat."

Sonny had forgotten about the flares. But he also wondered how his dad would see a boat in the distance come nightfall.

~

LUCILLE (SIXTEENTH HOUR IN THE OCEAN)

Lucille was fighting to stay awake. The slapping of the water against the makeshift raft was like the ticking of a clock. Twilight was coming on, and she wanted badly to curl up and sleep on the little raft, but there wasn't quite enough room. Her upper lip was chapped and burned, but she tried not to pick at it.

"I heard something," said Lucille.

The sailors perked up, searching the sky.

"An engine? I don't—" Burke began.

"Wait!" said Robello. They were silent again.

Sorli grabbed the loose tail of the flags and slipped a long board under it to raise it high above their heads, propping his elbows on the hatch cover next to Lucille.

"Yes!" said Robello.

Now Lucille could see a stubby aircraft coming nearer, its wings wobbling from side to side, signaling that the group had been seen. The aircraft seemed to take over all of her senses as it passed not far above the tiny raft, shaking her body with reverberations from its engines. The sailors were jubilant, and for a few moments all forgot the discomfort of skin rubbed raw by the salt water, unquenchable thirst, and stinging sunburn.

The plane circled back, and when it was almost overhead, a box popped out of the pilot's window, landing in the water not far from the group. One sailor paddled over to retrieve it.

For Lucille, the opening of the box was as exciting as Christmas morning. Inside were cans of water, candy bars, and skin cream for their sunburned faces. Despite their desperate thirst and a day without food, each waited patiently for a turn to help themselves to their share of the contents. More important than the comforting sips of water and the soothing skin cream was the assurance that help would be coming, that the outside world knew they were here.

The sailors were just as happy to be rescued as Lucille was, but they worried that Lucille's family might not have made it off the ship. Each man had his own remarkable survival story, like

Burke, who'd been dismayed at finding the ship sinking within 30 seconds of the first torpedo, and the sailor who had squeezed out of a porthole naked because he'd been in the shower at the moment of impact. None wanted to speculate on the fate of Lucille's family members: the energetic boy who had peppered them with questions, the stern father, and the kind mother who had been friendly to them all. Keeping a family intact through such a cataclysmic event would be impossible, and seconds spent trying to leave the ship could mean the difference between life and death. The men knew there would not be an accurate accounting of the 50 crew, six Navy Armed Guards, and six civilians for days to come.

20

A SILENT VIGIL

(DUSK INTO NIGHT)

INA (SEVENTEENTH HOUR IN THE OCEAN)

No plane appeared over Ina. Time dragged on, and she cried thinking of a life without Sonny, Lucille, and Ray. She briefly entertained the idea of letting go of the planks and slipping underwater to let the sea take her down. Anything to ease the pain.

She doubted she'd last another night at sea, not knowing what had happened to her children and husband. Then a prayer came to mind: "Dear Lord, I will not leave thee or forsake thee. Lord, I put myself in your hands," she murmured. "I lead my family to you; please protect them."

Dusk came, and still no sign of rescue. Ina second-guessed her decision to leave the sailors on the makeshift raft. The dark void of approaching night, with unseen sharks, terrified her. *With the sailors, I wouldn't have to face this alone*, she thought.

~

SONNY AND RAY (EIGHTEENTH HOUR IN THE OCEAN, NINETEENTH HOUR ON THE SHRIMPER)

Sonny had forgotten all about the sharks, but Ray hadn't. Ray still scanned the dark ocean around the raft for any sign of a fin. He wondered what to do if a shark appeared. If one came back, he thought he could use the strong light from a flare to scare it away. But they only had two flares.

The sun had set, but the survivors could still differentiate between the horizon and the ocean in the twilight. The prospect of another night in the water scared Ray to the core—not for himself but for Sonny, who was shivering in his arms. He regret-ted not waving in the plane. Now there was nothing he could do to change that decision.

Each time the raft rose to the top of a swell, all four survivors craned their necks to get a quick look at the horizon, hoping to see a boat. The captain estimated they had another 20 minutes before darkness would obscure their vision.

The adults were discussing whether and how to use the first of the two flares when Ray thought he saw a flicker of light in the distance. He didn't say anything, but instead waited for the raft to ride up the next swell so he could get another look.

At the top of the swell, he saw not only the light but the unmistakable silhouette of a boat!

"A shrimp boat is coming!"

Soon the men could see the outlines of other fishing boats heading in their direction.

In a few moments, one of the shrimp boats arrived at the raft, and the crew helped the survivors clamber aboard.

One of the first things Sonny noticed was the smell of food, and he realized how hungry he was. The crew wrapped him in blankets while his father asked if they had any news of his wife or Lucille. Unfortunately, they had not.

The survivors were given more water and small bowls of jambalaya. The shrimp boat captain continued searching the sea, using floodlights on the sides of the vessel and a third mounted on the top of the cabin that was aimed forward.

Sonny and Ray began a silent vigil, hoping against the odds that they would find Lucille and Ina, even though it was now dark. Ray thought about the two lucky breaks his wife and daughter would have needed to still be alive. First and foremost, they had to have made it past the staircase they were standing on when the *Heredia* lurched and the family was separated. Remembering his own struggle to break the glass and escape through a window, he knew their survival also depended on having been swept out of the sinking vessel. Finding a lifeboat or a raft from the ship also would have contributed to their survival. He recalled how quickly the ship went down, with the stern underwater almost immediately. He knew that the odds of Ina's and Lucille's survival were long. He didn't think anyone swimming in the ocean's cold water for more than 18 hours would be found alive.

When Ray was on the raft, he had put all his hope for his wife's and daughter's survival into the faith that they had been rescued well before Sonny and him. Now the bitter reality hit him that the likelihood of their being alive was remote. If they had been in a life raft or a lifeboat, surely the same plane that spotted his raft would have spotted theirs, and one of the shrimp boats in the fleet would have picked them up.

The despair Ray felt was crushing. He told Sonny it was just a matter of time before Ina and Lucille were found, but he was losing hope. Waiting was agony, so he told Sonny to lie down on a bunk, and he went up to the bridge. Ray asked the captain if he had his radio on. The captain said he did, explaining that a boat this small would not be a target for a U-boat. Ray asked if any of the other shrimp boats had picked up survivors. They hadn't, but the captain added that at least seven or eight boats were searching with their floodlights. Ray thanked him and returned to his son, hoping and praying for a miracle.

Sonny sat on a crew member's top bunk and stared out a porthole, and his dad did the same from a different porthole. The side floodlights illuminated an area of the sea about 25 feet out from the vessel. Sonny could not rejoice over his own rescue while thinking his mom and Lucille might be floating out there in the night . . . or worse.

The young boy trained his eyes on the dark water that shone under the floodlights, thinking that if he remained vigilant, he might be the one to spot them. Keeping his eyes open was another matter. Except for a brief period of sleep on the raft, Sonny had been awake since the first torpedo hit at 2 A.M. the prior night. He pressed his head against the glass and willed himself to keep looking, knowing his dad was doing the same.

After an hour of staring out the porthole at the black sea, Ray could stand it no longer and went back up to the helm. He wanted to make sure the shrimp boat captain would search through the night. Once assured, he returned to a bunk near Sonny and continued gazing out a porthole.

21

A WAVERING LIGHT

(DUSK INTO NIGHT)

LUCILLE (SEVENTEENTH HOUR IN THE OCEAN, EIGHTEENTH AND NINETEENTH HOURS ON A SHRIMPER)

The drone of the boat's motor was the most welcome sound Lucille had ever heard.

After the plane dropped supplies, the survivors had spent hours wondering when rescuers would appear. Conversation was muted as all listened intently for another engine sound from plane or ship, keeping watch as before at the crest of every swell. Finally, a wavering light appeared, and then an engine could be heard churning in their direction.

Silhouetted against the sky, the boat was small and low to the water, with long poles extending over the ocean on each side.

Several crewmen crowded the railing to see the people in the water. One was yelling instructions to the helmsman, telling him to cut the engine as they drew closer. It was a local shrimp boat, the *Shellwater*, with a crew from Morgan City.

Lucille was the first to be lifted from her flotsam perch and onto the deck of the trawler, which was cluttered with pails and piles of fishing net. Sorli was pulled aboard next, and Lucille saw him wince as he took off his life vest for the first time in more than 18 hours. His exposed skin was badly burned and raw from jellyfish stings.

Two crewmen carried the young girl down the companion-way, going first inside the pilothouse and down a small ladder. In a small bunkroom they let her stand on wobbly legs. A crewman asked her name and pointed Lucille to a basin to wash up while he laid some dry clothing on a lower bunk. Lucille's fingers were too raw and stiff to untie the knot her mother had firmly tight-ened on her life vest, so one of the fishermen cut it for her. When the sodden weight was lifted from her body, she felt weak and light-headed and began to fall. The two men caught her, placed her on the bunk, and then left to get her some food.

Lucille struggled to remove the pajamas she'd worn to bed. Her eyes teared at the memory of her snug stateroom in the *Heredia*, of the anticipation that home was so close at hand before the terrible hours in the water. *Where are Mother, Father, and Sonny?*

"Lucille?" said a voice at the door. It was Sorli. She finished pulling an oversized shirt on, feeling its roughness against her raw skin. He poked his head inside. "We're heading to land. The captain will try to contact other shrimpers and ask about your family."

Lucille was overcome with tears.

Sorli stepped forward to hug her, but when she put her arms around him, he tightened up because of his damaged skin.

After a small bowl of broth and some bread, Lucille stretched out on a bunk and slept while the boat's engines groaned through the water, rocking her to sleep.

~

INA (TWENTIETH HOUR IN THE OCEAN)

About that same time, in complete darkness, a voice in Ina's head said, *Look up in front of you.* She saw a light approaching her, and wondered if she was hallucinating. She had been in the ocean for 20 hours straight.

Squinting through her damaged eyes, Ina thought the light was on a mast of a ship. Shouting for help, she paddled on her board in the direction of the boat, now able to make out search-lights in addition to the light on the mast. In minutes, the boat was right on top of her, its noisy engines and the energetic voices of crewmen welcome sounds that cut through her exhaustion and despair.

Adrenaline overcame Ina's torpor, but she was physically unable to help herself get on board the shrimp trawler. Hands reached down toward her, but it was all she could do to lift her oil-drenched head.

One of the crewman shouted, "Get a rope! This person is alive!"

Ray and Sonny heard the commotion and ran topside. Sonny could see that someone was in the water. The person was dark-skinned and wore what looked to be a peacoat.

"Dad!" Sonny shouted. "Looks like they got one of the Filipino crew members."

Ray leaned as far as the could over the rail and saw a person covered in black oil whose hair was matted and thick with the gooey substance. He stared at the struggling survivor below.

Then Ray erupted. "Filipino, hell! That's your mother!"

A crew member threw a line to Ina, but she was unable to grasp it.

"Are you strong enough to let go of the board?" asked the crewman. Ina could only raise her hand toward the boat, looking up at it through one tearing eye.

The crewman reached down and grasped her arm, but it was still slick with heavy oil, and she slid back into the water like a seal. Ray also reached down to grab his wife, but she was just beyond his reach.

When the trawler captain approached to see why the survivor wasn't on board yet, he understood the situation immediately.

"Ma'am," he said, leaning over the side of the boat toward Ina, "would you agree to us using a rope to help you aboard? The oil is making it difficult, you see."

"Yes, if you would," Ina croaked.

A member of the crew quickly slid a rope under one of her outstretched legs and cinched it down with a knot. "Ready, Cap'n," he said.

"Now, ma'am, we will have you out of the water and in some dry clothes forthwith," the captain said, signaling the crew to haul Ina up using a pulley that pivoted over the stern of the trawler. She tried to grasp the rope with one hand while her leg was being pulled above the water, but the angle of the rope pushed her life vest against the lip of the boat. It was preventing her from being lifted higher.

"Down again, boys," said the captain. He reached out for the rope and moved it away from the boat, then signaled for the crew to try again. As Ina was raised out of the water, the captain grabbed her life preserver and pivoted his catch over the boat and landed her on the deck.

Ray and Sonny knelt next to her, clutching at her coat and tattered nightgown, helping her to sit up and then showered kisses on her face, which made their own lips black from oil.

Sonny, half crying with joy, choked out the words "Mom, you made it, you made it."

Ina managed a smile at hearing Sonny's voice. She was so exhausted that she bordered on unconsciousness. She wasn't sure where she was. She just knew that she was safe, and she had heard her husband's voice and her son's. She assumed Lucille was also with them.

Ray and some crew members picked Ina up and gently carried

her below to a bunk. The white sheets slowly turned black as oily water drained from her coat, nightgown, and skin.

Then, through blurred vision, Ina searched for Lucille. "Where is Lucille? Please tell me she is here!"

Ray and Sonny were silent. The captain of the vessel had already started motoring the boat toward land.

~

Just a half hour later, the radio aboard the boat that Ina, Ray, and Sonny were on crackled to life. "Captain, this is the *Shellwater*. Do you have a Raymond Downs on your boat? Tell him I have his daughter."

PART III

22

TRIUMPHANT
RETURN TO LORIENT

U-boat Commander Würdemann

While the Downs family was reunited and tried to reconstruct their lives, Commander Erich Würdemann served his country the best he could. After leaving the Gulf of Mexico, he moved off the U.S. coast on a northeast course, running on the surface with his diesel engines.

The crew of U-506 thought of home with each passing mile, relieved to be away from the terrible heat and humidity of the Gulf. They knew they were fortunate to have survived the high-risk hunts they conducted in the shallow waters off the Mississippi River. Had they been caught by aircraft or patrol boats, the crew might have had to blow up their own sub using demolition charges to keep it out of enemy hands. Their own fate was secondary: either go down with the U-boat or become a prisoner of war if they survived the sinking.

Having been successful in the heart of enemy waters for several weeks, they felt both accomplished and a bit lucky. It was likely the crew wanted to head straight to Lorient. They were traveling without torpedoes and expected to be in safe harbor within two weeks. Northeast of the Bahamas, however, lookouts spotted a steamer, and Würdemann ordered a change of course in pursuit.

This ship, the *Yorkmoor*, was British, and its crew was more seasoned than those of the American and South American vessels U-506 had previously hunted. These Brits knew exactly what to do when attacked.

The freighter had just left St. Thomas and was steaming to its discharge port in New York. Captain Thomas Matthews was in the chart room when Würdemann's first shell struck. Matthews immediately turned the *Yorkmoor* so that its stern faced where he believed the U-boat had attacked from. This maneuver would make his ship a smaller target—presenting his stern rather than the entire hull to the Germans—but still allow him to fire back.

The battle was on. Würdemann and U-506 were taking a bit of a risk by fighting it out on the surface with shells rather than torpedoes. If just one of the shells from the *Yorkmoor* hit U-506 on the surface, chances were the sub would not only lose the battle, but also eventually sink.

Soon one of the 105-millimeter cannon shells from U-506

penetrated the engine room of the ship. This hit seriously limited the *Yorkmoor*'s evasive maneuvers. Another shell hit beneath the ship's gun platform, blasting the primary gunner from his station. Somehow the injured gunner crawled back and continued firing. He directed his aim toward the muzzle flashes in the dark that signaled the location of the Germans.

On board the *Yorkmoor*, Captain Matthews was informed that the engine room was flooding fast. The lights had gone out, and the bow was beginning to settle. The Brits were still doggedly manning the deck guns, but they had lost sight of their target in the dark water. The British gunners could only wait, vulnerable and wounded, until the sub resumed shooting so they would know the direction in which to return fire.

When Würdemann had U-506 at a right angle to the freighter, he ordered a full artillery barrage. One of the German shells pierced the *Yorkmoor*'s hull, and a tremendous explosion ripped through the night when cold seawater flooded onto the red-hot boilers.

The duel was over. Matthews ordered his men to abandon ship. Forty-five sailors had to cram into a lifeboat built for 25. The second lifeboat was riddled with shrapnel and useless.

The sailors, drifting in calm seas over 400 miles from shore, had no prospects of help. But Captain Matthews made two quick decisions that likely saved lives. First, he instructed two men to repair the damaged life raft. Then he and the others began searching the floating debris for anything edible, finding food and fresh water. They stayed at the scene of the disaster for a full day and a half before the battered lifeboat was repaired and able to hold half the crew.

Six days later, off the coast of South Carolina, the castaways were seen by patrol planes and rescued. Thanks to the cool head of Captain Matthews, all 45 men survived. Their only injuries were severe sunburn, and rescue crews reported that "no one was hungry or thirsty when picked up."

~

While in the Bay of Biscay on June 11, U-506 had to crash-dive because of aircraft. An incoming message said what the crew already knew: "Expect increased air danger." In fact, British attacks on subs near Lorient had become so frequent that Dönitz issued new instructions to U-boats in the Bay of Biscay: Cross the bay submerged both day and night. The subs were allowed only a brief run atop the ocean under cover of darkness to recharge batteries. U-boats in the Bay of Biscay had become a rich focal point for the British Royal Air Force. And soon the planes would be joined by antisubmarine boats, making the bay one of the most dangerous places for a U-boat to pass through.

U-506 managed to dodge enemy aircraft, and after 71 days at sea, having traveled 11,249 nautical miles, it "made fast at Lorient Berth A1" on June 15. The celebration began for the conquering heroes. A band was waiting, and as U-506 fastened its lines to the concrete pen, the musicians struck up a lively tune.

Both Würdemann and Schacht were awarded the Iron Cross First Class. More significant than medals was that the two men would be forever known as commanders of the first U-boats that entered the Gulf of Mexico and sank ships near the mouth of the Mississippi.

MORGAN CITY,
LOUISIANA,
AND THE HOSPITAL

Sonny, get up. The boat's at the dock."

Sonny sat up and rubbed his eyes. Beyond the heavy wooden pilings visible through the porthole next to his berth were buildings and people. Deckhands were throwing heavy coils of lines to tie up the boat.

It was the scene Sonny should have experienced 24 hours previously, on the *Heredia*. It took him a moment to realize that the sunburn chafing his legs under the bedsheet, the scratches on his arms, and the growling hunger in his belly meant the ship-wreck ordeal hadn't been just a nightmare.

"Where's Lucille, Dad?" Sonny asked. He'd heard she was picked up by another shrimp boat but was anxious to see his family together again. He wanted to know they'd go back to a normal life after his surreal experience drifting on a raft at sea.

"Now, Sonny," Ray said, "here are some pants for you. They're not going to fit, but it's better than walking around in your undershorts. Just hike them up and hold on, and we'll see Lucille soon. I have to help your mother now; you go up on deck."

Sonny pulled up the light cotton pants and, despite being tall for his age, was nearly swallowed up by the fabric. A T-shirt on the bed was also for him, so he gingerly slid it on over his sunburned arms and shoulders, remembering briefly the way his father had demanded the captain's coat to protect him from the relentless sun. The memory caused a jolt of fear to shake his body. He put the thought of the barren sea baking in the sunlight out of his mind.

Sonny moved clumsily toward the companionway that led to the deck. One of the crewmen, a dark-skinned fellow with a crooked smile, greeted Sonny when he reached the deck. Soon more of the men gathered around and laughed and pointed at Sonny's unusual outfit. One ruffled his hair. Then a shout went up, and the men turned quickly, parting so Ray was able to come up on the deck carrying Ina. She was wrapped in a blanket, her eyes bandaged shut.

"Mama!" Sonny exclaimed. Ina held out a hand to him. Her skin was still grayish and discolored from the oil, her hair matted and wild. She looked a little scary, Sonny thought, but his heart nearly burst just to see her in his father's arms. He walked alongside his parents to the gangway. Looking up at the dock, he realized it was lined with police cars and ambulances. An orderly waited beside a gurney at the end of the ramp.

The boats had docked right in town, where the Atchafalaya River met Morgan City's Front Street. Sonny felt a little dazed by the jarring change from rocking boat to hard pavement. A row of buildings across the street offered shopping and restaurants. Behind him a tugboat growled against a barge as it headed up the brown river under a scallop-shaped bridge. More shrimpers were tying up at the dock, discharging sailors wearing partial uniforms and covered by blankets. From one boat a man's body was grimly passed to people on the dock.

"Sonny! Mama! Dad!" a high-pitched voice called out to them. Sonny's head whipped around.

"Lucille!" Sonny saw his dad's eyes light up and his mother suddenly looking stronger, a tearful smile spreading across her face. Lucille was a distance away, getting into a car with a tall, dark-haired man who waved enthusiastically.

Sonny thought about his brother, Terry, wondering if he'd say "shucks" when he heard about the ship getting torpedoed. Sonny wanted to ask if he could telephone Terry to tell him the story, but his dad was busy helping Ina get into an ambulance. Then Ray took Sonny's hand and led him to another waiting vehicle. Inside were Captain Colburn and Mr. Conyea. Ray hesitated outside the car, looking down at the men.

The captain wore his soiled white coat and pants, and he still had the binoculars around his neck. His face was a fiery red from sunburn, but he looked rested and composed. Mr. Conyea, in contrast, was exhausted and drawn, wearing a T-shirt and ill-fitting pants that Sonny realized must have been donated by the crew, like his own garments.

On the brief ride to the hospital, Sonny gazed out the window at the lush greenery of Morgan City, with the graceful gray Spanish moss hanging from trees. Bright flowers screamed at his eyes, which had been numbed by the days of gray-on-blue he'd experienced at sea. He was excited to see cars and trucks and people again, knowing he never had to get on another ship if he didn't want to.

~

The small hospital was bustling. Sonny was seated in a hallway outside a sterile examination room. Inside, behind the closed door, his mother and Lucille were alone, quietly talking as Ina waited for a doctor to discuss her recovery.

Sonny didn't understand why he had to wait outside, and he fidgeted in his chair, anxious for the door to open. He spent the time watching nurses dressed in white uniforms from head to toe move quickly up and down the hallway. Some of the *Heredia* sailors shuffled past in oil-soaked clothing, their arms and faces bright pink with sunburn; one still held a life jacket. Nuns in black habits flew past like blackbirds. One nurse leaned close to Sonny, took his temperature and listened to his heart, scribbling notes on a clipboard.

Sonny heard a familiar voice chirping from the examining

room. "That's my sister, Lucille!" he said. The nurse nodded and smiled. Sonny bolted to the doorway and saw Lucille leaning close to their mother, telling her about waving down the shrimp boat with flags on a long piece of wood. Ina's eyes were bandaged, but she was smiling, her hand stroking Lucille's hair.

The boy burst into the room and hugged Lucille, both of them crying and laughing at the same time, relieved to be together.

A couple of moments later, Ray stepped into the room, accompanied by a doctor in round spectacles. Ray suggested that the kids go to the cafeteria while he and Ina talked with the doctor.

A small cafeteria in the basement overflowed with hungry sailors, some sitting in the hallway outside. Their eyes brightened when they saw Sonny and Lucille, but the talk was subdued and smiles were rare. To Sonny, the food seemed endless, with glasses of milk, cups of juice, eggs and toast, grits and fruit salad. His stomach grumbled; he wanted to gobble all of it down.

"Not too much coffee now, you two," said a tall man with a mop of curly hair who was sitting at a table.

"Roy!" Lucille said. "We're so hungry we don't know where to begin. Remember what we talked about while we were floating? How we wanted chocolate cake and ice cream sundaes?"

Sonny recognized the handsome man as the ship's officer Mr. Sorli. The boy noticed that the sailor's face was red with sunburn. His arms were laced with grotesque red welts, as if he had been whipped.

When the children returned to the table with big plates of

toast and jam, the sailor laughed. "You must be from Texas, where everything is big," he joked.

"When we were on the raft, I found a banana in the water," Sonny said, remembering how he'd tried to hold on to the piece of green fruit, then lost it, then found it floating by again. He didn't think he'd ever eat another banana.

Despite all the people in the cafeteria, the room was hushed. Some of the *Heredia* crew members were still dressed in ragtag uniforms, tattered and dirty. Others wore borrowed clothing like Sonny's, mismatched and too big or too small. Sonny looked around at the men who had been so friendly aboard the ship and knew something had changed with the ship's sinking. Something about sitting there eating felt sad and lonely. Suddenly he wanted to be back with his mother and dad.

Seeing the sailors triggered something in Sonny, and he fought to hold back tears. He remembered the shouts for help in the night from both crew and passengers, remembered not knowing if he'd ever see his mother again. His eyes welled up, and his lip quivered. "I want to see Mama," he said quietly. Lucille took his hand and they walked down the hall.

When they reached the door of Ina's room, the doctor was gone, but they could hear Ray and Ina talking. Ina was speaking in a soothing voice about things working out, that the Lord had watched over them, but Ray's voice was stern. "I never should have signed that paper," he said. "All that work, all our savings, gone with the ship."

When Sonny and Lucille entered the room, Ray turned to

the window with his hands on his hips. The children noticed that one of Ina's eyes was now unbandaged.

"Betty Lucille, come here, I need a look at you," Ina said, turning her head oddly to see with her good eye. "Sonny, come around this side." The children crowded onto the edges of Ina's hospital bed so their mother could wrap her arms around them as Ray stood by quietly. Ina's left eye had a patch over it, and doctors planned to check it periodically to assess the damage from the ship's oil that had leaked into the ocean.

Just then a man interrupted, tapping on the door before he stuck his head in. He wore a crisp tan uniform and carried a clipboard. He wanted to talk to Ray about the ship.

Before Ray left the room, he told Ina he'd try to make a telephone call to Gainesville so their family would know the four of them were fine before any news about a shipwreck caused alarm.

Sonny asked his mom what the uniformed man wanted from his father. Ina explained that he was from the navy and was seeking information so other ships would not be torpedoed.

~

A couple of hours later, Ray returned. The children were curious about everything, but neither Ina nor Ray had the answers they sought. Had Mr. Beach survived the attack? How soon would Ina's eyes be clear? How long would they be at the hospital? How would they get home to Texas?

The children didn't know that the same questions gnawed at

Ina and Ray. The only question that was easy to answer was when Sonny asked if they would ever see the old family car again, which had been in the cargo hold of the *Heredia*. Ina smiled and asked Sonny to imagine the old Chevrolet with fish swimming around in it. She said they'd never have to change another tire on it again. That actually seemed funny to Lucille, who was glad to be rid of the old car. It wasn't so funny to Sonny, however. He made the connection between the sunken ship, the car, and so many other small items they'd left behind when they evacuated.

"My scooter!" Sonny wailed.

"Sonny, we can find you another scooter," Ina said. "What's important is that we're safe and sound."

"Roy and the other sailors said lots of people died. They're dead. The torpedoes killed them," Lucille said.

Ina explained that some of the sailors they knew had died in the shipwreck because they hadn't made it out of the ship in time or were too badly hurt to survive. It was the children's first experience with death, and Sonny suddenly understood the quiet cafeteria. He also thought back to his father's frantic, almost hysterical desire to swim back to the sinking ship to find Ina and Lucille. Sonny realized Ray had known people were dying at that moment.

Ray, who had been silent until now, took out a bag of clothes and shook out the contents at the foot of the bed. He held up a smock for Lucille and short pants and a shirt for Sonny. These were not new clothes, but they were clean and in the right sizes, which was a welcome change for Sonny, who'd been holding up his oversized pants for hours. Ina told him and Lucille to find a bathtub before they put the clean clothes on, and to be sure to scrub their hair to get all the salt out of it. Then they could go back to the cafeteria for a little more food.

When the children left the room, Ina took a deep breath. She began to sob. The reality of the situation was sinking in. She felt she'd watched the children age in front of her eyes as they realized that people had died, that they'd never see Sonny's scooter or their old clothes again. Crewmen who'd played checkers with them the day before were now dead. It was completely out of her control to protect them from this loss of innocence.

Without saying a word, Ray understood her churning emotions and sat on the bed to embrace her. He told her that her parents in Gainesville had received a reassuring telegram and that United Fruit had been notified and would arrange a meeting.

"What did the navy man tell you?" she asked.

"He said we can't share any details of the sinking yet. He just wanted to know what happened before and after the torpedo hit," Ray said. "I was asleep before, so I told him as best I could. If only they had let us off the ship in Corpus Christi the other night."

"I wasn't asleep," Ina said. "Before the explosion I couldn't sleep. I had the most awful feeling, Ray, like I knew something was going to happen."

"We were the lucky ones, Ina," Ray said. "Our whole family made it. All of us. There were sixty-two people on board that ship, and so far they've found just twenty-seven alive. A few who were badly injured got picked up by that seaplane and taken to another hospital. Mr. Beach wasn't found. I can't believe he went back to his cabin when they were telling us to evacuate. A few sailors may still be out there, but the navy doesn't think they'll pick up any more survivors."

Ray then announced that his decision to join the military was firm and nothing could change his mind. He explained that he'd seen the dead bodies in a room at the hospital, and witnessed the efforts to identify them. He had to get revenge.

24

RECOVERY

A woman knocked on the door of Ina's hospital room.
Ray was with his wife and he recognized the visitor, saying, "Mrs. Guidry, come in. Ina, this is Louise Guidry, who lives nearby and has offered to help."

The woman was petite and olive-skinned, with dark hair and bright eyes. She explained that the hospital was so overwhelmed by injured *Heredia* survivors that most of the other patients had been sent home to make room for them. She added that she and others from Morgan City had brought the sailors extra clothing from their families and were making food, too.

"We were so surprised to hear there was a family aboard," Louise cooed in her musical drawl. She said she would be happy to take the children during the day so Ina and Ray could rest. Then, noticing Ina's matted hair, the woman said she had something that would get the oil out.

Within an hour, Louise was hovering over Ina with tubs of shampoo, scrubbing and rinsing the sticky oil from her hair as the women chatted about their families, and a lasting friendship was formed. Louise had a granddaughter whose dresses fit Lucille perfectly, and she was able to find Ray, Sonny, and Ina an extra change of clothes for their eventual trip home to Texas.

Ina confided to Louise her worries about Ray's appointment to discuss their lost savings with the United Fruit lawyers. Their money had been locked securely in the ship's safe when the *Heredia* sank to the bottom. Ray had signed a waiver of liability when they boarded the *Heredia*, acknowledging that the ship's safe passage was not guaranteed and releasing the company from responsibility for loss of life or possessions. But when they'd boarded the ship under the Costa Rican sun, the possibility of falling prey to a torpedo attack had seemed as remote as thoughts of winter.

The family was now penniless; they were relying on the kindness of strangers for even the most basic necessities, such as clothing. Although Ina didn't specify to Louise the amount that had been lost, it had been an entire year's pay. That was the family's nest egg and prospect for a future home. They were starting from scratch again.

~

Four days after the rescue, the U.S. Navy ensign who had been in Morgan City to take survivors' statements allowed a newspaper reporter to visit the hospital. As soon as the reporter saw the Downs family, he knew he had struck gold for the front page: Sonny and Lucille were dimpled and smiling, Ray a hulking protector.

The story of the family's survival and photos of them smiling from the hospital room raced through papers in the region that were hungry for positive news. When interviewed separately, everyone from the *Heredia* praised Lucille and Sonny for their behavior during the ordeal. Ray and Ina were quick to publicly credit Roy Sorli with Lucille's safe return.

Underscoring the Downses' incredible night at sea and improbable reunion were the names and addresses of many Louisiana natives from the *Heredia* who had not made it home alive.

~

In Fort Worth, Texas, Ina's brother J. R. Evans picked up the Sunday paper six days after the torpedoing of the *Heredia* to find a familiar family smiling back at him. He sent a telegram to the hospital that read: "All of us are thinking of you every minute. When ready I will come after you if need be. If we can do anything let us know. Let us hear as soon as possible. Love JR."

Ina's father, John Evans, also saw the picture, and things started to make sense to him. He had been confused by a telegram he'd received a few days earlier that said the family was simply spending a week in a Morgan City hotel before returning to see Terry. The newspaper photo sent a shock wave through his body, and he immediately resolved to hear Ina's voice to get to the bottom of it. He telephoned the Morgan City hospital but was only allowed to speak to Ray after the navy ensign assigned to controlling the release of information had confirmed his identity. Mr. Evans was warned of repercussions if any secret details of the attack were discussed. The navy was still trying to squelch rumors and control information about U-boat activity despite civilian involvement.

Ray assured his father-in-law that he and the children were fine and that Ina's eye treatments were progressing well. Sight was being restored to her right eye, although she was still seeing double, and her left eye remained blinded by the oil and was of concern to the doctors. Ina's treatment included rest and rinses several times a day.

When Roy Sorli was allowed to call his fiancée, Heddy, in a Boston suburb, his delivery of the news was subtle. He didn't want to alarm her. "Well," he said, "I seem to have lost my boat." She never allowed him to go to sea again.

On Monday, May 25, a photo of the Downses was front and center in the New Orleans *Times-Picayune*. The children were smiling on either side of Ina, who had one eye bandaged, and Ray was behind them, his arms draped protectively around his family. The perky family photo offset other headlines on the page that blared war news: a successful Russian counteroffensive against the Germans, the possible sinking of a U.S. warship by an Italian submarine off Brazil, a Japanese plane smashing into an American ship.

Lucille's story about sharks tickling her feet caught the imaginations of many editors, who played up the peculiar anecdote in one newspaper after another. But the tale brought sadness to many households whose family members didn't have happy stories to tell. Ina received several letters sent to her in care of the Morgan City hospital by wives and mothers of the dead.

Mr. Beach's wife wrote to Ina and asked about her husband's last days.

"What do I tell her?" Ina asked Ray. "Should I say we told him not to go back to his cabin when the ship was sinking?"

Ray had no response. His mind was on the year's worth of savings that had sunk with the boat. The meetings with United Fruit were not promising; it seemed unlikely that the family would receive any compensation for their losses.

Soon another letter arrived at the hospital, addressed to Ina. It was from the mother of Frankie Platts, the very young member of the Navy Armed Guard, who hadn't seemed much older than the Downs children. The woman wrote that her husband was dead and her son was all she had left. The son had begged his mother to sign his papers to allow him to join the navy before he turned 18.

Despite her own shock and efforts to regain a little strength each day, Ina found the words to comfort the bereaved women. To Mrs. Beach she wrote, "You were in his thoughts to the very end," a kind way of acknowledging that he probably had returned to his cabin to retrieve the treasures he'd bought for his family.

For the distraught mother of the Navy Armed Guard Frankie Platts, she summoned a sunny image, writing, "Your son was wonderful to my children. He was a happy young man who played shuffleboard with them on deck when he was off-duty and never missed an opportunity to smile and pass the time. We've been told he did not suffer at the end but was unfortunately standing duty on a part of the ship that took a direct hit. I hope you find some comfort knowing that he brought happiness to others right up to the very end." In truth, Ina did not know how the boy had died. She even wondered if he'd been the young sailor holding on to the plank whose modesty about being naked in front of Ina had made him stay in the water. Ina couldn't be sure, because her vision had been so blurred by oil at that time.

Ina also wrote to Roy Sorli's fiancée to ensure that she knew how much the Downs family appreciated his caring for Lucille through the horrible ordeal. Lucille's stories about his humor and kindness, of allowing her to float atop the wreckage while he was stung by jellyfish and threatened by sharks for many hours, touched them deeply.

~

The Downses' mix of shock and elation receded after two weeks in the hospital. Sonny and Lucille were well fed and entertained by Louise Guidry, allowing Ina to rest and recover. The duo knew the route to Louise's house. They walked there eagerly each time they were invited to sample some of her fragrant dinners of étouffée and "snacks" of po' boy sandwiches on crusty bread.

Mrs. Guidry warned the kids about getting lost in Morgan City. She said it was bayou country, where the legendary Rougarou, a werewolf-like creature, roamed, looking for its next victims. Then she'd laugh and hug them close like they were her own children, sending them back to Ina and Ray with a sack of extra food.

Soon it was time for the family to move forward again. Ray and Ina had to reassemble their life, beginning with a train ride back to San Antonio and then to Gainesville to get Terry. They left the hospital with only the clothes they were wearing and the generous charity of the people from Morgan City. They bade an appreciative goodbye to the hospital staff and Louise, promising to write when they got to Texas. But Ray still had the U-boats on his mind, and Texas wouldn't be their last stop.

25

A FAMILY'S RESILIENCE

When Ina's treatment at the Morgan City hospital was complete, she still couldn't see out of her left eye, but the doctors had done all they could. The family returned to San Antonio with only a new set of clothes and train tickets. It was the only compensation they'd received from Ray's employer, United Fruit Company. All their possessions and savings had gone to the bottom of the Gulf with the *Heredia*.

Despite Ray's several meetings with company representatives regarding compensation, they would not budge. He had signed a waiver releasing United Fruit from responsibility when he and his family had boarded the ship, and the company held him to it.

The Downses had to be content with having escaped with their lives. They would have to try to rebuild their savings and replace the possessions that were lost.

Ray's resolve to join the service and do his part fighting the foes of the United States was stronger than ever. Once his family was safely back on land, he immediately sought to enlist in the Marine Corps. Despite his vigor and excellent physical condition, his age was a factor. At 37, he was too old for the marines.

But the coast guard needed as many men as possible. A major concern was that U-boats could be transporting spies and saboteurs to the United States. The few ships the coast guard had couldn't cover a thousand miles of coastline. Shore patrols were instituted, adding thousands of civilians with dogs and on horseback, ensuring nearly constant surveillance.

In June, the navy asked owners of small working boats and pleasure craft to assist with the coast guard's near-shore patrols. While 1,200 boat owners had already enlisted, another 1,000 were requested for this temporary reserve force. They would be equipped with "radio, armament, and antisubmarine devices." (On Cuba, author Ernest Hemingway had a similar idea. He had his private yacht outfitted with 50-millimeter guns and sought to hunt down U-boats the way he had once hunted big game in Africa. However, the famous writer spotted only one submarine that summer, and it was too far away to fire on.)

Ray was accepted by the coast guard in September 1942. His mechanical skills could have earned him a bigger paycheck in the private sector, but he was fixated on settling his score with the enemy that had nearly killed his family.

~

Ray reported for duty at the plush former Ponce de Léon Hotel in St. Augustine, Florida, which had been converted for coast guard training. He was fortunate to be able to fulfill his service close to his family. His rank was fireman first class, with duties including the operation and maintenance of boat engines. The job earned him a meager $213 per month, while other, less skilled coast guard enlistees were paid as little as $78 a month.

In St. Augustine, Ray learned to identify stealthy U-boats by their phosphorescent wake and the particulars of boat-engine repair. More important, he was able to channel his anger over the sinking of the *Heredia* into productive work.

While he trained in Florida, Ina and the children prepared for their new home. They had been staying with Ina's uncle and aunt in San Antonio. As arrangements were made for another Chevy that would take them across the Gulf States, they packed up the kitchen utensils, towels, and other necessities provided by generous friends and family. They had little to start with but looked upon the move as another adventure, even as the reality of their situation continued to sink in. Once, Terry asked his mother where his paint set was.

"I'm sorry, son. It was on the ship with everything else," she answered.

Their rented home in St. Augustine was among modest bungalows in a neighborhood just a few blocks from the Ponce de Léon, where Ray trained. He was soon assigned to a PT (patrol torpedo) boat patrol at the lighthouse station.

The three-bedroom home had the right amount of space for the family, and Ina immediately sought approval from the landlord to dig up a patch of grass and plant a victory garden. Terry found a job as a soda jerk, and Lucille, now 12, began babysitting. Everyone pitched in to ease the family's financial burden, which was their way of sharing their father's sense of duty. Sonny was taught to run laundry through the wringer on the home's old washing machine and to wipe down the clotheslines before hanging the family's shirts and pants out to dry. He also hoed the weeds in the garden and helped Ina sterilize canning jars when it was time to put up the vegetables they'd grown.

When school started, Sonny was a little shy. He squirmed when the teacher introduced him to his new third-grade classmates, explaining he was from Texas.

"You're from Texas? Are you a cowboy?" one boy sneered. The label stuck, branding him "Cowboy" around school and making Sonny feel stigmatized. He began to crave the time he had with his dad and Terry on weekends, which usually revolved around playing sports. It was an investment in time that paid dividends later in life.

The monthly pay of an enlisted man didn't go far with three growing children to feed. Ina was unable to work full-time as a seamstress until her eyes had completely healed, yet she took on the challenge of scrimping and saving. She made the best of the government's newly instituted ration system, which allowed each family only limited quantities of goods—from car tires to sugar and shoes.

"You're spending too much money on food," the children heard Ray say one night.

Never one to back down, Ina responded, "Well, we can't just do without it."

After duty hours, Ray returned home to echo Ina's emphasis on education, and the children complied, bending closer to their books and composition pages when he appeared. Ray spent more time reading the Bible and began teaching Sunday school at their church, changes the children surmised were related to the *Heredia* sinking. But his children knew, too, that his sleep was racked with nightmares, and Ray might have been seeking peace from a higher source for that affliction as well.

The *Heredia* and its aftermath slowly faded from family conversation, partly to avoid inflaming Ray's terrible nightmares. The family had a new sense of purpose: fighting the enemy by participating in the war effort on the home front. But the wrenching experience would always be part of their history and sense of strength and resilience.

FEATURES INDEX

.23 Financial 24-25
.28 Radio 29
.18 Society 21-22
.12 Sports 14-16
.20 Woman's Page ...26

The Times-Picayune

Exclusive Pictures by AP WIREPHOTO
Associated Press News

NEW ORLEANS, MONDAY, MAY 25, 1942

Entered N. O. Postoffice as Second-Class
Matter Under Act of March 3, 1879

U.S. W
Little tempe
peratures Su
same day la

D AT SEA; EWS CLAIM ING WARSHIP

INDUCTION PLAN MAY SOON PERMIT 'SENDOFF' PARTIES

Draftees, Beginning July 16, Will Get Two-Week Furlough

Patriotic "sendoff" demonstrations for men inducted into the army now may be planned with certainly because of a new induction procedure arranged by the war department and the selective service system, Brigadier General Raymond H. Fleming, state director of selective service, announced Sunday.

The new procedure, which becomes operative July 16, assures a two-week furlough, at government expense, for every selectee accepted by the army and sets a date for each group to report back to its local board headquarters for transportation to an army reception center, General Fleming said, adding that this is the date for which local demonstrations should be planned.

"Since all of the men assembling at the local board office after a furlough period have been accepted for military service and ordered to active duty," General Fleming said, "once will be faced with the embarrassment of returning home as rejected following such ceremonies."

The new arrangement replaces the present system of granting inductees 10-day furloughs upon re-

The Downs Bob Up Again After Sub Attack in Gulf

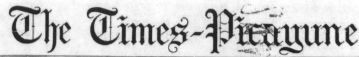

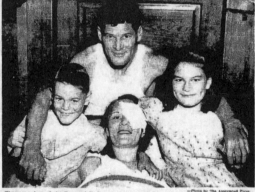

These members of the Raymond P. Downs family of San Antonio, Tex., were happily reunited Sunday at Morgan City, where they related their experiences in what the navy described as the "worst disaster" yet reported in Gulf submarine attacks. The children, Betty Lucille, 11 years old, whose feet were "tickled by sharks" as she floated on a hatch cover, and Raymond, Jr., 8, "acted like grown people."
—Photo by The Associated Press.

NAZI SUBMARINE SAILOR 'SALUTES' SHIP'S SURVIVORS

Crewman Waves German

Family Is Reunited After Torpedoing of Ship, Fight to Beat Off Sharks in Gulf

Father, Mother, Two Chil-

RUSSIANS PUSH (HEAPS OF GERM AS BITTER FIG

JAP PLANE FALLS; HITS ALLIED SHIP; 100 ARE RESCUED

Injured Survivors Taken Off by Warship; Fire Put Out; Disabled Craft Sunk After Assistance Arrives

(By The Associated Press)
Allied Headquarters, Australia, May 25 (Monday)—An Allied ship under attack by Japanese planes several hundred miles off Australia caught fire when an enemy craft, winged by anti-aircraft guns, crashed amidships, General MacArthur's headquarters announced today.

An Allied warship rescued 100 survivors, many of them injured. Practically all men on the deck of the attacked ship were injured and many below suffered severe steam scalds and burns.

The planes attacked the vessel from three sides simultaneously. Decks were machine-gunned and three bomb hits were scored before the ship's funnel.

The ship began to list immediately and some of the crew were lowered in lifeboats. Others stayed with the ship and had the flames subdued by the next day.

An Allied flying boat signalled that help was en route and later

Reds Overcom Tank-Plane Air Fightin Allied Bom!

The mighty Russ Sunday night across t a determined Germa Kharkov, pivotal city Soviet offensive.

Dispatches from hills strewn with pile line rolled back a con venkova sector, wher desperately to reliev communications and

The German higl had been encircled so was almost wholly d employ when victory

The Russian acc holding firmly to the attacks were lessenin Marshal Semeon Tim

The changes at tl tanks inched forwar claims to have passe attack in the Izyum-

Jap
In other parts of between the Chinese opening several offen

PASTORS DEMAND

EPILOGUE

THE END OF U-506

In July 1943, U-506 had engine trouble while crossing the Bay of Biscay near Spain. An American B-24 Liberator found the U-boat sitting on the surface and dived out of the clouds, successfully attacking and sinking the submarine with depth charges. Several crewmen who were on deck managed to survive after several days in a life raft, but Würdemann and about 44 others died that day. Schacht and his entire crew of U-507 had met a similar fate 300 miles off Brazil in January 1943.

These scenes played out repeatedly from 1943 to the war's end in 1945 as the Allies combined technologies to better track and stop U-boats. The tide was turning against the Germans' most effective war machines.

THE WAR GRINDS TO A CLOSE

By the spring of 1945, it was clear that the Germans had lost the war. Within months the Nazi leadership crumbled. On April 30, just before Hitler died by suicide, he named Admiral Dönitz his successor—a surprise because Dönitz had not spoken to Hitler face-to-face in more than nine months.

On May 7, just a week after Hitler's suicide, Dönitz approved the surrender of Germany. He sent a message to the Kriegsmarine, thanking them for fighting like lions while telling them to surrender. The war at sea had been relentlessly brutal: more than 2,600 Allied merchant ships were sunk, along with 175 Allied naval vessels and 784 of the fleet of 1,162 U-boats.

Dönitz went on trial before the International Military Tribunal in Nuremberg, Germany, which determined punishment for war crimes. Dönitz, aided by loyal members of the Kriegsmarine, was found guilty of some charges but served just 10 years in prison, while other German commanders were executed for the atrocities they designed and carried out.

The final tally of the war showed that approximately 40,000 men served on German U-boats, but only a quarter of them survived the war. Thanks to the Allies' superior airpower and submarine-detection technology, the Atlantic Ocean is littered with sunken U-boats.

THE DOWNS FAMILY

After Ray's two-year stint in the coast guard at St. Augustine, the Downs family was again on the road, searching for the right combination of employment and luck that would enable them to rise above their meager circumstances. From St. Augustine, they packed up and went west again, to Texas. Ray had a job with a railroad, and they would be closer to family.

Their new home, however, turned out to be a motel near the railroad yard in bustling Abilene. The two-bedroom efficiency was a tight squeeze. The children—now ages 16, 14, and 10—tried to put a good face on starting at yet another new school. Terry immediately fell in step with other football players, but Sonny remained scrawny and somewhat shy. At age 14, athletic Lucille was still playing ball with the boys, strong-willed enough to withstand the "girls can't" attitude of teen boys.

~

After just a few months in Abilene, the Downs family was on the move again, this time "home" to San Antonio. Ray went to work for the U.S. Postal Service, and Ina, with her sight restored, returned to sewing and baking. They lived just a few blocks from the home they had left in 1941.

It was here that Sonny received his first and only failing grade in school: His teacher, Mrs. Hall, assigned the students to write a nonfiction story about the war. When Sonny turned in an essay about the torpedoing of the *Heredia*, his teacher chided him for making it up and etched a big red *F* on the page. Ina was not happy to hear about it. She marched down to the school to set that teacher straight.

Ever busy working as a soda jerk and trimming neighbors'

lawns, Terry saved his earnings in hopes of going back to St. Augustine to work for a summer on a friend's shrimp boat, but family finances remained tight. When Terry was ready to use his savings for a train ticket to Florida, Ina had to admit that his money had been spent on other necessities, dashing Terry's dream.

Sonny delivered newspapers, carrying them on his bike before school. He knew the story of Terry's savings being depleted, so he decided to keep his cash in a sock rather than giving it to his mother to hold. He had to move the sock frequently to avoid impromptu "loans" to his siblings.

In high school, Terry grew to over six feet tall, broad-shouldered and strong, turning heads on the playing fields. He decided to attend Baylor University on a football scholarship and study dentistry. He married twice, had two sons, ran his dentistry practice in San Antonio for 50 years, and headed the Texas Dental Association.

In time Sonny also grew to six feet tall, and his desire to play baseball was challenged by his basketball coach, Day Brandt, who noted his ability to sink shots from any point on the basketball court. Brandt counseled Sonny to focus solely on basketball, and Sonny agreed.

~

When Lucille graduated from high school, she received a heart-felt letter from Roy Sorli and his wife, Heddy, congratulating her and reminding her that she had been a brave young lady. In fact,

Ina stayed in touch with the Sorlis for many years following the *Heredia* torpedoing.

Lucille became an executive secretary, working for the Federal Reserve Bank branch in San Antonio for most of her career. She married twice and had four children with whom she was always active, including playing tennis and swimming. Lucille is remembered for her beauty, larger-than-life personality, and the strong will that anchored her children's lives, yet she also struggled with crippling depression. Sadly, she died during surgery at the age of 67.

Roy Sorli, the Norwegian second mate of the *Heredia*, returned to the arms of his sweetheart, Heddy, near Boston. He honored her wish and didn't return to sea, spending the rest of his life working as a union carpenter and raising two children. He had a small boat but stayed close to shore and taught seamanship as flotilla commander of the local U.S. Coast Guard Auxiliary. The Merchant Marine Meritorious Service Medal he received for saving Lucille hung in his home, but he rarely spoke of it.

Both Ray and Ina Downs lived long lives after their harrowing experience, but they eventually lived apart. After divorcing, both of them continued to live and work in San Antonio, Ina as a seamstress and Ray for the state employment commission.

~

Sonny's survival at sea was just one chapter in a rewarding life. He attended the University of Texas at Austin on a basketball scholarship, racking up high points as a rare ambidextrous player. He still holds the school's career scoring average (22.3 points per game) and single-season scoring average (26 points per game) records, more than 60 years after graduating.

Sonny was drafted by the St. Louis Hawks of the new National Basketball Association in 1957 but never played in the league. He joined the army and began selling insurance policies to his fellow soldiers, eventually becoming a top producer. He married Betty Gayle Lowther of San Antonio and has three sons. Today Sonny lives in Massachusetts and is still a top salesman in the financial industry.

~

In 1992, an oil slick appeared in the Gulf of Mexico, and many potential sources were investigated. It was eventually determined that it was the remaining fuel oil seeping out of a weathered wreck called the *Heredia*. The rusting hulk sits mostly intact 80 feet underwater, a silent legacy of a terrible war and a family's resilience.

A NOTE FROM THE AUTHORS

The young boy in Ray "Sonny" Downs is still evident when he tells the story about sitting on the life raft with his father, distracted from his fear and hunger by playing the seagull game. Emotions still well up when he speaks about seeing his mother hauled aboard the shrimp boat, covered in sticky oil. Without his clear, poignant recollections of these events, this book would have no heart.

The era we write about is in the past, but the Downs family's struggle to stay together and seek the best opportunities for financial advancement still resonate today. To this end, we sought to portray Ray and Ina Downs, the parents, as honestly as possible, using their own words from family documents and their children's memories. They were simple people who took a chance in pursuing the most basic dream: providing their children with a better future. In the end, they were never wealthy but left indelible impressions of determination, perseverance, and resilience on their children.

We learned that U-boat commanders and sailors did not all believe in the Nazi regime. Reading their war diaries gave us a glimpse into their decision-making, their leadership, their focus on destroying the enemy, and at times even their compassion. We hope this book paints a balanced picture of them.

As we were writing the book, we wondered at what an inspiring family the Downses were. Each member showed a resilience that was off the charts, both during their ordeal at sea and in the months that followed. It was an honor to write their story.

BIBLIOGRAPHY

INTERVIEWS AND LETTERS

Several interviews with Ray "Sonny" Downs. Ray also wrote a description of the attack and his survival ordeal.

Interviews with Terry Downs

Several letters written by Ina Downs while in Colombia. Ina later dictated a description of her survival story to her friend Joan Swanson.

Ina's audio recording of her voyage on the *Heredia* and her ordeal at sea, which included a discussion of Lucille's experience as told to her

Letters to Ina from the parents of a sailor killed on the *Heredia*

Letters from Roy Sorli to Lucille and Ina

Some of our best information came from the Germans on U-506 (see "Documents" section)

BOOKS

Blair, Clay. *Hitler's U-Boat War*. New York: Random House, 1996.

Buchheim, Lother-Gunther. *U-Boat War*. New York: Bonanza Books, 1986.

Busch, Rainer. *German U-Boat Commanders of World War II: A Biographical Dictionary*. Annapolis, MD: Naval Institute Press, 1999.

Christ, C. J. *WWII in the Gulf of Mexico*. Houma, LA: CJ Christ Publishing, 2005.

Cremer, Peter. *U-Boat Commander*. Annapolis, MD: Naval Institute Press, 1984.

Darman, Peter. *Warships and Submarines of World War II*. London: Grange Books, 2004.

Doenitz, Karl. *Memoirs: Ten Years and Twenty Days* (English translation). New York: World Publishing, 1959.

Duffy, James P. *The Sinking of the* Laconia *and the U-Boat War.* Santa Barbara, CA: Praeger, 2009.

Dunnigan, James, and Albert Nofi. *Dirty Little Secrets of World War II.* New York: William Morrow, 1996.

Feldman, George. *World War II Almanac.* Detroit: Gale Group, 2000.

Frank, Wolfgang. *The Sea Wolves.* New York: Ballantine, 1955.

Gannon, Michael. *Operation Drumbeat.* New York: Harper and Row, 1990

Gildea, Robert. *Marianne in Chains.* New York: Metropolitan Books, 2003.

Groom, Winston. *1942.* New York: Atlantic Monthly Press, 2005.

Hastings, Max. *Inferno.* New York: Knopf, 2011.

Hickman, Homer. *Torpedo Junction.* Annapolis, MD: U.S. Naval Institute, 1989.

High Command of the German Navy. *U-Boat Commander's Handbook.* Translated by the U.S. Navy. Gettysburg PA: Thomas Publications, 1989

Hough, Richard. *The Greatest Crusade: Roosevelt, Churchill and the Naval Wars.* New York: William Morrow, 1986.

Hoyt, Edwin. *U-Boats Offshore.* New York: Stein and Day, 1978.

Huettel, Wilfred Chuck. *War in the Gulf of Mexico.* Santa Rosa Beach, FL: Hogtown Press, 1989.

Jackson, Robert. *Kriegsmarine: The Illustrated History of the German Navy in World War II.* Minneapolis, MN: Zenith Press, 2001.

Jacobsen, Hans Adolf, and J. Rohwer. *Decisive Battles of WWII.* New York: G. Putnam and Sons, 1960.

Kimball, Warren F. *Churchill and Roosevelt: The Complete Correspondence (Volume 1, Alliance Emerging, October 1933–November 1942).* Princeton, NJ: Princeton University Press, 1984.

McKay, Ernest. *Undersea Terror.* New York: Julian Messner, 1982.

Mercey, Arch, and Lee Grove. *Sea, Surf and Hell: The U.S. Coast Guard in World War II.* New York: Prentice-Hall, 1945.

Miller, Nathan. *War at Sea.* New York: Scribner, 1995.

Moore, Arthur. *A Careless Word . . . A Needless Sinking.* Kings Point, NY: American Merchant Marine Museum Press, 1983.

Morison, Samuel Eliot. *History of United States Naval Operations in WWII: The Atlantic Battle Won*. Chicago: University of Illinois Press, 1956.

Niestle, Axel. *German U-Boat Losses During World War II*. Annapolis, MD: Naval Institute Press, 1998.

Offley, Ed. *The Burning Shore*. New York: Basic Books, 2014.

Padfield, Peter. *Dönitz: The Last Fuhrer*. New York: Harper & Row, 1984.

Peillard, Léonce, and Oliver Coburn. *U-Boats to the Rescue: The Laconia Incident*. London, Jonathan Cape, 1963.

Prien, Gunther. *U-Boat Commander*. New York: Award Books, 1976.

Rohwer, J., and G. Hümmelchen. *Chronology of the War at Sea 1939–1945*. New York: Arco Publishing, 1974.

Rohwer, Jürgen. *Axis Submarine Successes, 1939–1945*. Elstree, UK: Greenhill Books, 1998.

Savas, Theodore P. *Hunt and Kill: U-505 and the Battle of the Atlantic*. New York: Savas Beatie LLC, 2004.

———. *Silent Hunters: German U-boat Commanders of WWII*. Boston: Da Capo Press, 1997.

Shaw, Anthony, and Peter Darman. *World War II Day by Day*. London: Brown Reference Books, 1999.

Showell, Jak P. Mallmann. *U-Boat Commanders and Crews*. Wiltshire, UK: Crowood Press, 1999.

Trevor-Roper, H. R. *The Last Days of Hitler*. New York: Macmillan, 1947.

Vause, Jordan. *Wolf: U-Boat Commanders of World War II*. Annapolis, MD: Naval Institute Press, 1997.

Werner, Herbert A. *Iron Coffins*. New York: Holt, Rinehart and Winston, 1969.

Westwood, David. *The U-Boat War*. London: Conway Maritime Press, 2005.

Wiggins, Melanie. *Torpedoes in the Gulf*. College Station: Texas A&M University Press, 1995.

———. *U-Boat Adventures*. Annapolis MD: Naval Institute Press, 1999.

Williamson, Gordon. *Grey Wolf: U-Boat Crewman of World War II*. Oxford, UK: Osprey Publishing, 2001.

Willoughby, Malcolm. *The U.S. Coast Guard in World War II*. Annapolis, MD: Naval Institute Press, 1957.

Documents

Confidential Summary of Anti-Submarine Action by Aircraft (ASW-6), report completed after 2LT Salm's flight report of U-506 sinking in July 1943, uboatarchive.net.

Dönitz War Diary: "War Diary and War Standing Orders of Commander in Chief, Submarines," Des Führers/Befehlshaber der Unterseeboote (F.d.U./B.d.U.), Naval History and Heritage Command, Washington, D.C., and uboatarchive.net.

Enclosure to U-506 War Diary, 3rd Patrol, Labeled "Report on the Reception and Care of *Laconia* Shipwrecked," National Archives and uboatarchive.net.

Hartenstein, Werner, U-156 War Diary: "U-Boat Kriegstagebücher (KTB)" for 4th Patrol, National Archives and uboatarchive.net.

Schacht, Harro, U-507 War Diary: "U-Boat Kriegstagebücher (KTB)" for Patrols 2, 3, 4, 5, National Archives and uboatarchive.net.

"Summary of Statements by Survivors, SS *Heredia*, American Passenger and Cargo Ship, 4732 GT, United Fruit Company, New Orleans, LA," U.S. Navy, National Archives.

"U-506 Interrogation of Survivors," C.B. 04051 (75)," Naval War Division (of the U.K), London, August 1943, U.K. National Archives.

Würdemann, Erich, U-506 War Diary "U-boat Kriegstagebücher (KTB)" for Patrols 1, 2, 3, 4, 5, National Archives and uboatarchive.net.

Newspapers

"21 Lost as One Craft Escapes; 36 Die on Other." *Times-Picayune*, May 24, 1942.

"87 Land in Brazil from 3 Lost Ships." *New York Times*, August 15, 1942.

"Allston Mate of Torpedoed Ship Tells of 16-Hour Struggle in Gulf." *Boston Daily Globe*, May 26, 1942.

"America Solving Problem of Sub, Says President." *Times-Picayune*, May 22, 1942.

"American Troop Convoy Reaches Port in Ireland." *Times-Picayune*, May 19, 1942.

"Battle for Oil Speeds War to Supreme Crisis." *Times-Picayune*, May 14, 1942.

"Battle Is Fiercer: Nazi Chutists and Tanks Fail to Halt Red Army Before Kharkov." *New York Times*, May 19, 1942.

"Both Sub, Shark Hit Him, Relates Survivor of Ship." *Times-Picayune*, May 18, 1942.

"Catalina Flying Boat Praised on Submarine Guard." *Times-Picayune*, May 14, 1942.

"City Still Glows in Haze of Light After New Dimout." *New York Times*, May 19, 1942.

"Convoy Is Largest: First Armored Forces of Our Army Land in British Isles." *New York Times*, May 19, 1942.

"Declaring War on U.S. Hitler's Biggest Blunder, Louis Lochner Discloses." *Times-Picayune*, May 16, 1942.

"Doolittle, Record Maker During Peace, Leads U.S. Tokyo Raid." *Times-Picayune*, May 20, 1942.

"Dutch Ship Sunk, Gun Crew Among 14 Losing Lives." *Times-Picayune*, May 13, 1942.

"First Hospital in Patterson." *Morgan City Daily Review*, September 1, 1978.

"Fourth Gulf Ship Hit by Torpedoes Towed into Port." *Times-Picayune*, May 15, 1942.

"Greatest Boom to Follow War, Banker Believes." *Times-Picayune*, May 19, 1942.

"Higgins Reveals Plans to Speed Output of Ships." *Times-Picayune*, May 14, 1942.

"Injured Seaman Saved by U-Boat as Vessel Sinks." *Times-Picayune*, May 24, 1942.

"M. C. General Hospital Closes with Many Laurels to Its Credit After 15 Years of Service to This Area." *Morgan City Daily Review*, November 25, 1955.

"Navy Seeks 1,000 Boats for U-Boat Patrol; Relaxes Requirements, Offers Commissions." *New York Times*, June 28, 1942.

"Nazi Saboteurs Planned to Blow TVA and Hell Gate, Clark Reveals." *New York Times*, November 8, 1945.

"Neutral Mexican Ship Sunk as Axis Torpedo Crashes into Lighted Flag on Side." *Times-Picayune*, May 15, 1942.

"Oceaneering Divers to Plug Sunken Submarine's Oil Leak." *Morgan City Daily Review*, August 14, 1992.

"Rationing of Spending by Public Urged to Bar Inflationary Buying." *New York Times*, May 19, 1942.

"Reds Near Kharkov, Allies Bomb Japs." *Times-Picayune*, May 17, 1942.

"Roosevelt Weighs Pipeline to Ease Gasoline Shortage." *New York Times*, May 19, 1942.

"Sinkings by U-Boats Cut Sharply Under Navy's Coastal Convoying." *New York Times*, August 15, 1942.

"Slick: Oil Seeping from Ship Sunk in WWII." *Times-Picayune*, August 14, 1992.

"Stalin's Army of Rapists: The Brutal War Crime That Russia and Germany Tried to Ignore." *Daily Mail* (UK), October 24, 2008.

"Story of WWII Spies Lives On in Maine." *Bangor Daily News*, July 15, 2003.

"Submarine Bill Is Signed by President." *Times-Picayune*, May 14, 1942.

"Through Rose-Colored Glasses." *Times-Picayune*, May 20, 1942.

"U.S. Ship Among Three Lost." *New York Times*, July 8, 1942.

"U-Boats Attacked 111 Ships and Sank 92 Along Gulf-Sea Frontier During the War." *New York Times*, June 4, 1945.

"U-Boat Skipper Recalls Good Hunting Off East Coast." *The Baltimore Sun*, November 2, 1992.

"U-Boats Sink Vessel, 57 Lose Lives." *Times-Picayune*, May 24, 1942.

"Vast Funds in Gold, Silver and Securities Assembled at Corregidor, Brought Safely to America." *Times-Picayune*, May 16, 1942.

"War on Submarine Gains, Says Vinson; House Chairman Voices His Confidence of Ending Threat to Shipping." *New York Times*, June 8, 1942.

"Young Navy Blimp Crews Itch to Get U-Boat on Daily Tours." *New York Times*, February 12, 1942.

MISCELLANEOUS

"Thunder in the Gulf." *Louisiana Life*, Summer 2000.

"Torpedoed Once—Bobs Up in USCG." Coast Guard newsletter article about Ray Downs, 1943.

"War Diary: The Submarine Situation." Eastern Sea Frontier, April 1942.

Warnock, Timothy. "The Battle Against the U-Boat in the American Theater," pamphlet, Air Force Historical Research Agency, 1994.

WEBSITES

ahoy.tk-jk.net/macslog/IndextotheSubmarineArticl.html.

americainwwii.com/articles/sharks-in-american-waters.

baseballinwartime.com

brownmarine.com

cv6.org/company/muster/organization.htm#Grades

history.army.mil/documents/mobpam.htm

history.com

history.navy.mil/content/history/nhhc/research/library/research-guides/german
    -navy-u-boat-submarine-headquarters-war-logs-from-world-war-ii.html

history.navy.mil/research/library/online-reading-room/title-list-alphabetically
    /g/german-espionage-and-sabotage/eastern-sea-frontier-war-diary.html

www2.census.gov/prod2/statcomp/documents/1946-04.pdf

nationalww2museum.org/learn/education/for-students/ww2-history/ww2-by
    -the-numbers/us-military.html

navycs.com/charts/1941-military-pay-chart.html

nps.gov/casa/planyourvisit/upload/World%20War%202.pdf

pbchistoryonline.org/page/the-enemy-presence-german-u-boats

raf.mod.uk/history/bombercommandtenthousandbomberraids3031may.cfm

salutetofreedom.org/nc.html

staugustinelighthouse.org

uboat.net

uboataces.com

uboatarchive.net

uboatsbermuda.blogspot.com/2014/01/all-143-u-boat-patrols-off-bermuda-1942
    .html

ubootarchiv.de/ubootwiki/index.php/U_506

usmm.org/wsa/shiploss.html

usmm.org/battleatlantic.html

wikipedia.org/wiki/Operation_Torch

wreckhunter.net/u-boats.htm

ACKNOWLEDGMENTS

The idea for this book came about in a surprising way. I was hired to speak about leadership to employees at a financial company when I met attorney Jim Hoodlet, a fellow fisherman.

When Jim and I were on a boat off Cape Cod, Jim hooked me the same way he later hooked a couple of big fish. He mentioned Ray "Sonny" Downs Jr., a friend and top financial adviser who had survived a U-boat attack in the Gulf of Mexico when he was just eight years old. Soon afterward Jim followed up with information about the *Heredia* sinking, a 1942 newspaper article about the Downs family, and a photo of the vessel. The story was intriguing.

Coauthor Alison O'Leary and I were surprised to learn that the *Heredia* was far from the only ship torpedoed in the Gulf, and realized most Americans know little about this part of World War II history. After we met Ray "Sonny" Downs, we knew he was someone we could work with, so we dived in. Ray's brother, Terry, was a wonderful source of family documents and memories, and we are indebted to Valerie Cousino,

Lucille's daughter, for the audiotape of Ina and Louise Guidry talking about the *Heredia* sinking and the weeks afterward in the hospital.

~

Another indispensable source for the book was Jerry Mason, who created the website uboatarchive.net and is a wealth of information. He answered every question, no matter how trivial or complex. Jerry, a graduate of both the U.S. Naval War College and the U.S. Air Force Air War College, retired from the U.S. Navy in 2005 as a captain after a distinguished career as a naval aviator. We can't thank him enough for his patience and help.

Many other people went out of their way to offer us a helping hand or to help make this book a reality, and some are listed here: publisher and editor Christy Ottaviano (who has expertly guided me on several books), associate editor Jessica Anderson, and publicist Kelsey Marrujo.

DON'T MISS THESE OTHER TRUE RESCUE STORIES

A New York Times Bestseller

An Amazon Best Book of the Month

A Junior Library Guild Selection

"A thrilling, harrowing account of disaster and heroism."
—Kirkus Reviews

An NCSS Notable Social Studies Trade Book

A Cybil's Children and Young Adult Literary Award Finalist

A Junior Library Guild Selection

"This true story reads like a thriller."
—Booklist

An Amazon Best Book of the Month

A Junior Library Guild Selection

"Reads like a thriller, suspenseful and ultimately tragic . . . Riveting."
—Kirkus Reviews